CONTEMPORARY'S

AMAZING CENTURY

BOOK ONE

1900 TO 1929

D1300893

Developed by Contemporary Books, Inc., and General Learning Corporation, Northbrook, Illinois

Copyright © 1992 by Contemporary Books, Inc.
All rights reserved

No part of this publication may be reproduced, stored in a retrieval system, or transmitted in any form or by any means without the prior written permission of the publisher.

Published by Contemporary Books, Inc.
Two Prudential Plaza
Chicago, Illinois 60601-6790
Manufactured in the United States of America
International Standard Book Number: 0-8092-4020-3

Published simultaneously in Canada by
Fitzhenry & Whiteside
195 Allstate Parkway
Markham, Ontario L3R 4T8
Canada

Library of Congress Cataloging-in-Publication Data

Amazing century.
      p.   cm.
   Includes indexes.
   Contents: bk. 1. 1900–1929—bk. 2. 1929–1945—bk. 3. 1945–1960—
   ISBN 0-8092-4020-3 (pbk. : v. 1).—ISBN 0-8092-4018-1 (pbk. : v. 2).
   ISBN 0-8092-4017-3 (pbk. : v. 3)
      1. United States—Civilization—20th century.
   2. Civilization, Modern—20th century.
   I. Contemporary Books, inc.
   E169.1.A47186   1992
   973.9—dc20   91-35292
                                                              CIP

Editorial Director
Caren Van Slyke

Executive Editor
Laura Ruekberg

Assistant Editorial Director
Mark Boone

Managing Editor
Alan Lenhoff

Project Editor
Pat Fiene

Associate Editor
Miriam Greenblatt

Editorial
Chris Benton
Sarah Conroy

Art Director
Ami Koenig

Editorial Production Manager
Norma Fioretti

Research
David Bristow
Sam Johnson
Terese Noto
Therese Shinners
Betty Tsamis
Deborah Weise

Cover Design
Georgene Sainati

Cover Photo
UPI/Bettman: handcoloring
by Scott Kitzerow

To Our Readers

The coming of the automobile and the airplane . . . the tragedy of world war . . . the rise of sports stars Jack Johnson, Babe Ruth, and Helen Wills . . . the glamour and excitement of Hollywood and the first movies . . .

In the pages of this book are some of the biggest news stories of their day—stories that touched the hearts and minds of our grandparents and great-grandparents. The photographs and stories in this book reach out to us. They tell about people and events that have helped to shape this century—and make our nation what it is today.

Though you may not know all the faces and places, you'll recognize many of the stories behind them. You'll see that today's news stories have their roots in the past—and that we have many things in common with the people who came before us. We learn from their tragedies and benefit from their triumphs.

In pictures and in words, each of the books in the *Amazing Century* series highlights a different time period in this century. See for yourself. Thumb through the pages of this and all the *Amazing Century* books, and discover the way we were.

The Editors

Money Matters

Crime, Punishment, and the Law

Science and Technology

T I M E L I N E

1903
Wright brothers
successfully
fly
engine-driven
airplane

1901
President
McKinley
assassinated

1906
Major
earthquake
hits
San Francisco

1909
National
Association for
the Advancement
of Colored People
(NAACP)
is founded

Robert Peary
reaches
North Pole

1908
Ford Motor
Company
introduces
Model T

1914
Assassination
of Austrian
crown prince
triggers
World War I

Panama
Canal
opens

1913
16th Amendment
establishes
income tax;
17th Amendment
sets up rules
for number and
election of
senators

25th–31st U.S. Presidents

William McKinley	Theodore Roosevelt		William Taft	

1900	1901	1902	1903	1904	1905	1906	1907	1908	1909	1910	1911	1912	1913	1914

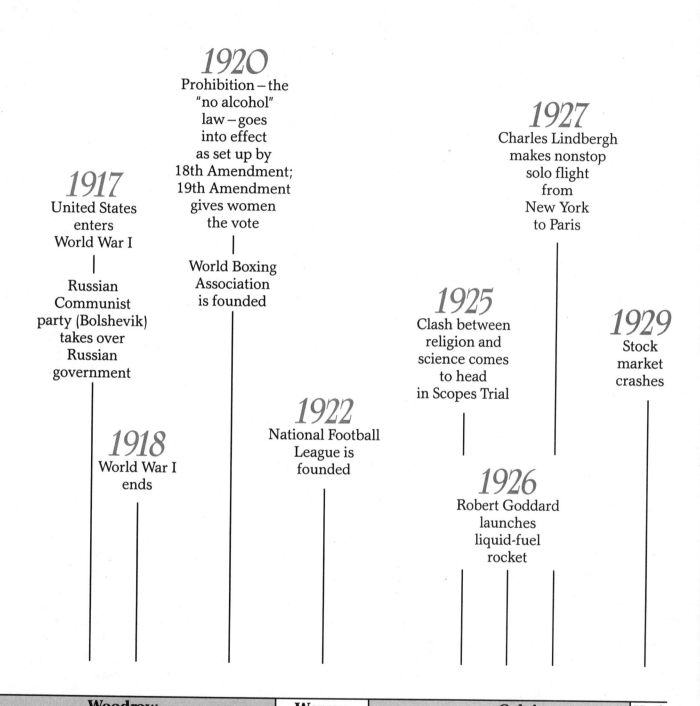

1917
United States
enters
World War I

Russian
Communist
party (Bolshevik)
takes over
Russian
government

1920
Prohibition – the
"no alcohol"
law – goes
into effect
as set up by
18th Amendment;
19th Amendment
gives women
the vote

World Boxing
Association
is founded

1927
Charles Lindbergh
makes nonstop
solo flight
from
New York
to Paris

1925
Clash between
religion and
science comes
to head
in Scopes Trial

1929
Stock
market
crashes

1918
World War I
ends

1922
National Football
League is
founded

1926
Robert Goddard
launches
liquid-fuel
rocket

Woodrow Wilson	Warren Harding	Calvin Coolidge	Herbert Hoover

1915	1916	1917	1918	1919	1920	1921	1922	1923	1924	1925	1926	1927	1928	1929

The Progressive Era: 1900–1917

What did Americans think the 20th century would be like? Most thought the new century would be a time of change and progress – a progressive era.

Americans knew that the country faced serious problems: crowded slums, unsafe and filthy workplaces, child labor, and corruption in government, to name a few. But most Americans were also hopeful. They believed that the United States had the vision and power to solve its problems.

Americans from all walks of life called themselves Progressives: business leaders, politicians, social reformers, writers, and workers. The Progressives shared certain goals. They wanted to improve living and working conditions in the cities and to clean up government. They also wanted laws to control big business.

Big Business: Progressives' Target

By 1900, the United States had more factories – making more products – than any other country in the world. Americans moved from the countryside to cities to work in these factories. Immigrants came from overseas to work in them too.

Many of these factories were owned by a few big companies. While big business had created many jobs for people, the jobs often came with low pay, long hours, and dangerous working conditions. Giant companies also had a great deal of power over city and state governments. The owners of these companies fought against reform laws that might cost them money. Progressives believed big business had too much power. Their motto was "Give the government back to the people."

People's President

Theodore Roosevelt brought Progressive ideas to the White House. Vice president under William McKinley, he became president in September of 1901, after President McKinley was assassinated. Teddy Roosevelt was the right man for the times. He was smart, optimistic, and full of energy. Roosevelt came from a rich family, but he believed in justice for both rich and poor. He believed it was the government's job to make sure people got justice. He said that he wanted to "put a stop to abuses of corporations" and make even the

5:30 P. M.

ROOSEVELT TAKES OATH FIRS

Proba
L

Buffalo This Afternoon on

Roosevelt wanted to make sure that big corporations stopped breaking antitrust laws, which made it illegal for one company to control a whole industry. Roosevelt and his administration also tried to make business owners settle problems in ways that were fair to workers. For example, in 1902, Roosevelt took steps to end a long strike against the coal industry. He set up a board to listen to both sides of the story—the workers' side and the industry leaders' side. He then made the industry leaders follow the board's recommendations. The workers won higher wages and shorter hours. The Roosevelt administration also supported laws to keep children from working long hours, laws to protect women workers, and laws to clean up

As 26th president of the United States, Theodore Roosevelt (left) brought Progressive ideas to the White House. He believed in equal justice for the rich and poor.

"biggest business man in the country conform squarely to the principles laid down by the American people."

To cut back the power of big business, Roosevelt's administration took some companies to court.

The Muckrakers

For some working-class Americans in the early 1900s, eating dinner could be dangerous. Was meat on the menu? There was no telling if it was fresh or clean. It may have been processed in dirty surroundings and doctored up to look fresh. How about some milk? If a family was lucky, the milk was *only* watered down. Many dealers added chalk or plaster to give the milk they sold a better color, and some dairy farmers sold milk from cows too sick to stand without help. Other store-bought foods were also impure. Butter was sometimes mixed with mashed potatoes or rotting animal fat.

Coffee might be full of ground peas, nutshells, or flour. Nothing was "guaranteed" safe for eating.

In 1906, Americans were horrified by what they read about Chicago's meat-packing factories in Upton Sinclair's book *The Jungle*. They read about filthy cutting rooms and sick workers. Sinclair wrote: "There were those who made the tins for the canned meat. . . . Their . . . hands were a maze of cuts, and each cut represented a chance for blood poisoning. There were men who worked in the cooking rooms, in the midst of steam and sickening odors. . . . In

these rooms the germs of tuberculosis might live for two years, but the supply was renewed every hour."

Descriptions like this made readers sick. They also made readers angry. Later that year, Congress hurried to pass the Pure Food and Drug Act and the Meat Inspection Act.

Upton Sinclair was one of many writers and journalists who fought for social and political reform. President Theodore Roosevelt called them "muckrakers." Their goal was to dig up and expose the "dirt" and dishonesty in American business and government.

The camera was a powerful tool for "muckraking" reformers. Photographer Lewis Hine and others took many photographs of children at work. Pictures like this convinced many Americans to support child labor laws and other laws protecting workers.

unsanitary conditions in the food industry. With Roosevelt in the White House, the terrible living conditions of the city's poor people began – slowly – to improve.

Roosevelt's actions earned him enemies in the business world. But many Americans supported him. He ran for president in 1904 and was elected by a large majority. His supporters hoped Roosevelt would help make the American Dream come true for everyone. ■

Some people think the U.S. government is too involved in consumer protection. They dislike the power of government agencies like the Consumer Product Safety Commission (CPSC). They think agencies interfere with business in America. What do you think? How involved should the government be in protecting consumers?

THEN & NOW

Modern-day muckrakers are known by different names – some are "consumer advocates"; others are "investigative reporters."

Ralph Nader is a well-known consumer advocate. He informs consumers about misleading advertising and unsafe products.

Reporter Bob Woodward gained national attention with his book *All the President's Men* in 1974. The book told about the Watergate scandal of President Richard Nixon's administration. It contributed to the growing public anger against the president. This anger caused Nixon to resign the

presidency in 1974.

More recently, Woodward has written about the administration of former President Ronald Reagan. In his book *Veil: The Secret Wars of the CIA 1981–1987*, he charges that the administration approved the Central Intelligence Agency's use of bribery, deception, and even assassination in countries such as Nicaragua, Libya, and Iran.

These modern muckrakers are controversial figures. Some say they are trying to hurt certain people to further their own political views. Others say that they fill an important role – as "watchdogs" for the public.

WAR in Europe

At the beginning of the 1900s, Americans believed that wars were a part of the past – not part of their future in a new century. They didn't expect or want war. As one popular song put it, "I didn't raise my boy to be a soldier."

But there were signs of trouble in Europe. To build up their power, nations had been forming alliances – promises to defend each other if war broke out. On one side was the German empire – Germany, Austria-Hungary, and their other allies. These nations came to be known as the Central Powers. On the other side were France, Great Britain, and Russia. They came to be known as the Allies. Both sides had been increasing their armies and building more ships. Europe was turning into an armed camp.

The United States knew that trouble was brewing in Europe. But most Americans did not want to get involved in "Old World problems." An ocean

New York Tribune

WEATHER
FAIR TO-DAY; PARTLY CLOUDY
MORROW.

IV....No. 24,784.
[Copyright, 1914.
By The Tribune Association.]

NEW YORK, WEDNESDAY, AUGUST 5. 1914.
• • •
PRICE ONE CENT In City of New York, Newark, Jersey City and ELSEWHERE TWO CENTS.

NGLAND DECLARES WAR ON GERMANY;
BATTLES BEGIN ON LAND AND SEA;
KAISER LOSES WARSHIPS OFF ALGIE

EUROPE NOW AFLA
WITH FIVE NAT
IN SUPREME

LATEST NEWS OF THE WAR.

London, Aug. 4.—Great Britain declared war on Germany at 7 p. m. More than 500,- under arms in Great Britain. House of Commons votes $525,000,000 for "emer- ... at 7 p. m., "a state of war exists." ... when military aims

AR OF SIEGE GUNS
BRUSSELS OF

Kaiser Refuses to Respect Belgia
d at 7 p. m. Breaks Off

SATURDAY, MAY 8, 1915.

VELT RAPS O. P. DOOR

1,216 LOST LIVES ON LUSITANIA; FEW OF THE AMERICANS SAVE

UP IN WATER

OFFICIALS CALL SITUATION GRAVE

Washington Does Not Con-Anxiety Over Results

VICTIMS' BODIES FILL WAREHOUSE

ADDITIONAL DEAD LIE HOTELS

Funerals of Most of them Held Sunday—Children C. One Another Still Unide tified.

The *Lusitania*, a British ship, was sunk by a German submarine.

separates the United States from Europe, and so Americans believed they could live in peace despite the problems in Europe.

War Breaks Out

On June 28, 1914, Archduke Francis Ferdinand, the crown prince of Austria, was killed by an assassin in the city of Sarajevo, Serbia (now Yugoslavia). This was the spark that would set Europe on fire. One month later, Austria attacked Serbia in retaliation for the archduke's death. One by one, the other nations of Europe were drawn into the fight by the alliances they had formed.

Russia and France supported Serbia in its battle against Austria. Germany, allied with Austria, prepared for war against Russia and France. When Germany invaded Belgium and moved toward France, Great Britain fulfilled its promise to France by declaring war on Germany. Alliances had forced many nations to become part of the fight. Instead of a "little war" between Austria and Serbia, Europe had a "Great War" that lasted more than four years.

America Stays Out—for a While

President Woodrow Wilson didn't want the United States to fight in Europe. In 1916, he was reelected on the slogan "He kept us out of war." Wilson told Americans that war "cannot touch us." He warned the nations of Europe that America would remain neutral.

But England, France, and the other Allies made it hard for the United States to stay out of the war. Americans got most of their war news from British and French reports. These dramatic stories were designed to build support for England and France in their battle against Germany. They told shocking (and untrue) tales about Germans killing babies and women, and Germans making soap from the bodies of enemy soldiers.

Germany also made it hard for the United States to stay out of the war. In

February of 1915, Germany declared the waters around the British Isles to be a war zone. It announced that it would use submarines to sink enemy ships and neutral merchant ships traveling in these waters. Some of the merchant ships were American. They were carrying goods to be sold to England and other Allied nations. Some of the ships also carried American passengers.

Germany argued that it *had* to stop supplies from reaching countries it was fighting. President Wilson warned that the United States would break off diplomatic relations with Germany if German submarine attacks killed American citizens or sank American ships. In May of 1915, 128 Americans died when a German sub sank the British ship *Lusitania*. And in March of 1917, German submarines sank four American merchant ships.

The Russian Revolutions

While the war in Europe continued, something else was happening that would have far-reaching effects. Russia was turning to communism.

It was February 23, 1917 (by the old "Julian" calendar, used in Russia until 1918). In the capital city of Petrograd (now St. Petersburg), a long line of women had been waiting in the bitter cold all night, hoping to buy bread. Russia had plenty of food. But the country's railroad system was so inefficient that people in the large cities often went hungry. On this day, the women were told there was no bread to be bought. Desperate, they began smashing store windows in search of something to eat.

Later the same morning, workers from the city's textile and metal-working plants went on strike. They paraded through the streets, carrying banners that read, "We want bread." The next day, the number of strikers

doubled. Now their banners also read, "Down with the war." The strikers thought the war against Germany was starving Russia.

On February 25, some 250,000 people jammed the streets of Petrograd. Offices, shops, and schools were closed. No newspapers appeared. Even the streetcars stopped running.

On February 26, the strikers spent the day urging the 160,000 soldiers in the local army barracks to support them: "Join us, comrades. Put down your rifles or give them to us."

On February 27, several regiments of soldiers mutinied and joined the workers. Together, they stormed Petrograd's main prison and set free political prisoners. That night, a provisional government—a government meant to be temporary— was organized. It asked the czar, or emperor, to give up his power. Three days later, Czar Nicholas II stepped down from the throne. The February revolution was over. The Provisional

Czar Nicholas II with his five children. All were executed by the Bolshevik government in 1918.

Demonstrators (above right) being shot at with machine guns during a protest in July 1917. Vladimir Lenin (above) works in his office after taking control of Russia.

Government, headed by Alexander Kerensky, ruled Russia. But it would not hold power for long.

Enter Lenin

Eight months later, a second revolution took place in Russia. The October revolution created what was the Soviet Union, known officially as the Union of Soviet Socialist Republics (USSR).

The October revolution was led by the Bolsheviks under Vladimir Ilyich Lenin. Lenin believed that people were poor and hungry because a ruling class owned the factories and the land. Lenin wanted the government to run the economy. And he wanted the Bolsheviks to run the government. Unlike the leaders of the Provisional

Government, he was not interested in democracy.

Also, Lenin wanted to end the war against Germany. The Russian army had suffered horribly because the czar's government had managed the war badly. Soldiers at the front lacked food and boots. One out of four did not even have a gun. Soldiers had to pick up weapons from their dead comrades. As a result, by the middle of 1915, 3.8 million men had been killed. And the casualties kept mounting.

Day after day, Lenin and the Bolsheviks called for "Peace! Bread! Land!" In October, the Bolsheviks won a majority of the seats in the Petrograd and Moscow soviets. *Soviets* were

The New York Times.

"All the News That's Fit to Print."

NEW YORK, FRIDAY, NOVEMBER 9, 1917.—TWENTY-TWO PAGES.

LXVII.. NO. 21,839.

THE WEATHER

EVOLUTIONISTS SEIZE PETROGRAD; KERENSKY FLEES; PLEDGE IS GIVEN TO SEEK "AN IMMEDIATE PEACE" ITALIANS AGAIN DRIVEN BACK; LOSE 17,000 MORE M

MINISTERS UNDER ARREST

'RUSSIA OUT' S
SPARTANBURG

men's and soldiers' Delegates told The Associated Press today that the object of taking possession of the posts and telegraphs was to thwart any effort the Government might make to call the capital. The

Council Welcomes Lenine.

The Petrograd Council of Workmen's and Soldiers' Delegates held a meeting at which M. Trotzky made his declaration that the Government no longer some of the Ministers had the preliminary

organizations of workers and soldiers that had been formed in the major cities. On the night of October 26, the Bolsheviks overthrew the Provisional Government and seized power. Only six lives were lost in the battle. In March 1918, they signed the Treaty of Brest-Litovsk with Germany, which pulled the Soviet Union out of the war. Then they turned their attention to building the world's first communist state.

The U.S. Goes to War

Meanwhile, in April of 1917, the United States had declared war on Germany and joined the Allies. "The world must be made safe for democracy," President Wilson had said.

Could the United States help win the war for the Allies in Europe? The country was not well prepared. The U.S. Army was small. It had only about 200,000 soldiers, and most of them

"The world must be made safe for democracy."

— President Woodrow Wilson

President Wilson addresses the U.S. Congress, asking for a declaration of war.

Maps illustrating the boundaries of the European nations before the war and (far right) after.

TROOP STRENGTH:
Armed Forces in World War I (in millions)

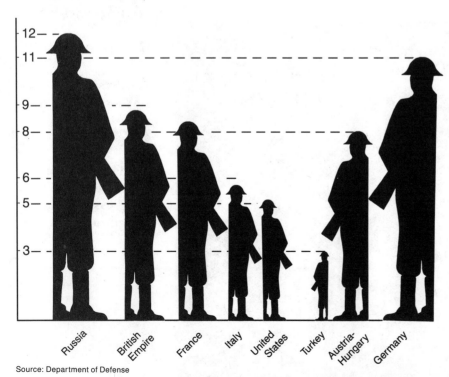

Source: Department of Defense

were new, with little training. The United States worked quickly to build its forces. By the end of 1917, nearly 10 million American men were signed up for military service. American factories also supported the war effort, working hard and fast to produce equipment and supplies.

By the end of 1917, the armies of Germany, France, Great Britain, and other European countries had lost hundreds of thousands of men. The fresh troops from America—and the supplies they brought—gave new life to the Allies. By the summer of 1918, more than a million American soldiers were fighting in Europe, and Germany began to crumble. Germany formally surrendered on November 11, 1918—only 19 months after the United States had entered the war.

Making Peace
President Wilson sailed for Paris to help make the peace. He wanted to be

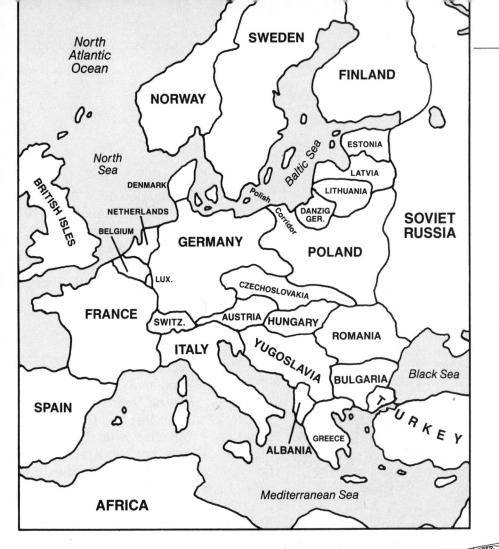

sure that his ideas became part of the Treaty of Versailles—the Allies' peace agreement with Germany.

Wilson believed his most important idea was to create the League of Nations. The League—like today's United Nations—would have members from many countries. It would help countries settle problems peacefully, without war.

Most European leaders wanted to punish Germany for the war. Wilson, on the other hand, wanted "peace without victory." He did not want Germany destroyed. European leaders insisted that Germany be punished but agreed to make the League of Nations an important part of the peace treaty.

Many Americans didn't like the idea of the League of Nations. They viewed the League as another kind of alliance. After the problems that alliances had caused in Europe, Americans were not eager to form new alliances with European countries. They were afraid that the United States would keep on having to fight in Old World wars if it joined the League.

After the peace talks in Europe, Wilson brought the Treaty of Versailles back home. He had to get the U.S. Senate to approve the treaty and America's membership in the League of Nations. But Wilson's opponents worked hard to turn public opinion against the League.

Years after the war was over, political cartoons asked what its purpose had been.

THIS IS **WHAT** HAPPENED IN THE GREAT WAR------

LET'S SEE, WHAT WAS THE WAR ABOUT, ANYWAY?

SEARCH ME!

HOW DID IT START?

IT WAS SOMETHIN' ABOUT AN ARCHDUKE OR SOMETHIN'

AND NOW, ELEVEN YEARS LATER, THERE ISN'T ONE MAN IN TEN THOUSAND WHO CAN TELL YOU **WHY** IT HAPPENED!

BENNY SENT ME

The Senate voted down the Treaty of Versailles twice—in November of 1919 and March of 1920. It would not approve the treaty because membership in the League was part of the agreement. Wilson had lost. The United States would never become a member of the League.

"Normalcy"

In 1920, a presidential election took place. The Republican party chose Warren G. Harding, a senator, to run for president. Harding told the American people that what they needed now was "not heroism, but healing"—a return to what Harding called "normalcy." To many Americans, this meant that Harding would keep America out of foreign quarrels—and let the United States get back to the good, prosperous times before the war.

Harding was elected president in a landslide victory. The American people had chosen "normalcy." ∎

Some Americans did not want the United States to fight in World War I. They believed that we should not get involved in "other countries' problems," even if those other countries were our friends. They felt that we should not fight unless our own country were under attack. Today, some Americans feel the same way. For example, some Americans believe that we should not be involved in the conflicts among Arab nations—or in the conflict between Israel and some Arab nations.

What is your opinion? Do you believe the United States should help defend other countries? Or should we fight only if our own country is under attack? What are your reasons for feeling as you do?

The Immigrant Experience

A man remembers the day he arrived in America as a 10-year-old boy: " 'Mountains!' I cried to my brother. 'Look at them!' 'They're strange,' my brother said. 'Why don't they have snow on them?' He was craning his neck and standing on tiptoe to stare . . . at the New York skyline."

People are right to call the United States a nation of immigrants. Since the

An immigrant mother posing with her children. Many people came to America hoping to find jobs and escape poverty and hunger.

Ellis Island

Beginning in 1892, Ellis Island, off the shore from New York, was the first stop for most immigrants. American inspectors checked for disease or mental illness and asked many questions: Where are you going? Do you have a job skill? Do you have money? For many people, Ellis Island was a terrifying place—because the inspectors had the power to send people back where they came from.

Ellis Island was closed during the 1950s. But in 1990 it opened again—as a museum. Visitors who come to Ellis Island today can learn about the history of immigrants in the United States.

1600s, waves of immigrants have helped to shape the country we know today. Between 1860 and 1915, almost 30 million immigrants came to the United States.

Why did people come to America? Times were bad back in the "old country." People came to America to escape poverty, hunger, or joblessness. Sometimes they came to avoid serving in the army or to find freedom of religion. All the immigrants thought they could find a better life in the United States. They saw America as the land of opportunity.

Where did they come from? From 1860 to 1890, most immigrants came

Ellis Island, New York, where immigrants from nations throughout Europe got their first taste of America.

Immigrants arrive at Ellis Island carrying their belongings.

from England, Ireland, Germany, and the Scandinavian countries (Sweden, Norway, and Denmark). These people had a history and a culture much like that of the early pioneers who built the United States. Many of these immigrants already spoke English. Most of them were farmers—and America in those days was still a nation with plenty of land left to farm. For all these reasons, this "old" wave of immigrants found it easy to become part of the American community.

But after about 1890, a new wave of immigrants began to arrive. They came from Italy, Russia, Poland, and other parts of Eastern Europe. Others came from China and Turkey. The "new immigrants" had a harder time becoming part of American life. Most of them did not speak English. And while many of them were country people, America had little land left to farm. The old immigrants were already farming most of the available land, and they did not welcome new farmers.

So new immigrants crowded into big cities: New York, Boston, Chicago, Detroit, San Francisco, and others. In 1900, one-third of the people living in New York City had been born in some other country.

FOREIGN-BORN POPULATION IN THE UNITED STATES IN 1920

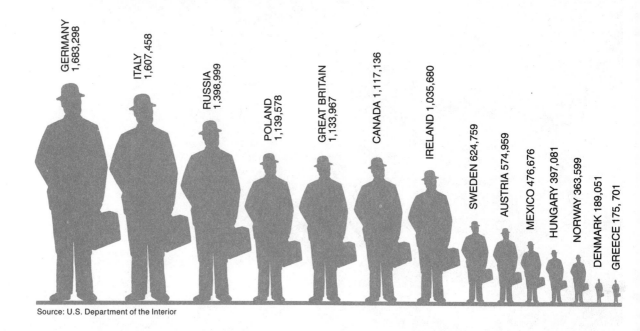

GERMANY 1,683,298
ITALY 1,607,458
RUSSIA 1,398,999
POLAND 1,139,578
GREAT BRITAIN 1,133,967
CANADA 1,117,136
IRELAND 1,035,680
SWEDEN 624,759
AUSTRIA 574,959
MEXICO 476,676
HUNGARY 397,081
NORWAY 363,599
DENMARK 189,051
GREECE 175,701

Source: U.S. Department of the Interior

An Immigrant Family's First Years in America

What happened to these new immigrant families *after* they came to the United States? Usually, their first home would be in a big-city neighborhood where friends or relatives had already settled. Immigrants from one country often formed their own neighborhoods within the city – a Chinatown or a Little Italy. "Many Italians hardly know they are outside their native land," said one visitor, "because here they have everything Italian."

The new immigrants joined a church or synagogue like the one they had left behind and bought newspapers printed in their own language. Some adults never learned to speak more than a few words of English. But their children – who, by law, had to attend school – soon learned "American" ways and left their parents' language and customs behind. Immigrant children often acted as interpreters for their parents.

Life could be hard. Some adults of the family took jobs in factories or in "sweatshops." Others walked the streets as peddlers – selling anything from bananas to old clothes. Sometimes mothers and children worked at home, rolling cigars or making paper flowers. The hard (and low-paid) work of the new immigrants helped make America's great industrial growth possible.

Many new immigrants died from overwork and other problems that come with poverty. But many others improved their lives. A Russian-born peddler remembers: "Many of the men who carried packs on their backs . . . became very rich. They learned American business ways. Some of the largest department stores in the country were started by men who peddled with packs on their backs."

Immigrants on the Lower East Side of New York City kept parts of their native cultures, but they also began to enter the mainstream of American life.

Fear Sets In

Some Americans were afraid of the huge numbers of immigrants coming into the country. They believed these people were bringing foreign ideas that would hurt the country. They said the government should stop letting so many new immigrants into the United States. In 1917, Congress passed an immigration law to cut down on the number of new immigrants. The law had many strict rules. Among them was one that said adult immigrants must pass a reading and writing test — in their native language or in English — or be sent back where they came from. ■

Many Americans did not welcome the "new" immigrants who came to the United States between 1900 and 1917. The immigrants were faced with physical exams, literacy tests, and quotas.

Ask a recent immigrant to the United States about his or her experiences. Did the person have trouble getting into the United States? Did he or she feel welcome? What special problems has the person had to solve?

Do you think most Americans welcome immigrants today? Are some groups better thought of than others? Why do you think this is so?

Black Rights: First Stirrings

During the Progressive Era, one group of Americans did not benefit much from reforms: African-Americans. In all parts of the nation, blacks lived in segregated neighborhoods, separate from whites. In many places, blacks were kept from voting by laws that made them pay a special voting tax or take a reading test. Black schools were given little money for books and equipment. Black workers were often paid lower wages for the same work that whites did.

Working for Equality

In the early 1900s, many important leaders in the black community worked hard to change these conditions. But these leaders did not always agree on what was the best way to improve the lives of black people.

Booker T. Washington, a longtime black leader, believed that black Americans needed good job training and "the opportunity to earn a dollar in a factory." William E. B. Du Bois, a young black teacher and writer, did not agree with Washington. Du Bois said that young blacks should not be trained just for jobs as factory workers or farmers. He said that blacks should learn the things they needed to enter a "higher civilization." Du Bois believed that black students should study science, literature, politics, philosophy – anything they wanted. And he thought blacks had to fight racism if they wanted a better place in society.

Marcus Garvey

Another black leader, Marcus Garvey, thought black Americans should return to Africa and create their own new nation. He believed blacks would never be treated fairly in a white country. Garvey attracted many blacks to his "Back-to-Africa" movement. By 1923, Garvey claimed he had 6 million followers. But his movement failed when he ran out of money – and found that most of his followers didn't really want to go back to Africa.

Booker T. Washington (left) and W. E. B. Du Bois (right), African-American leaders who fought for justice for blacks.

The Ku Klux Klan in 1920. The KKK carried out acts of violence against African-Americans and other minorities.

In 1905, W. E. B. Du Bois called for selected black leaders to meet near Niagara Falls, Ontario. The purpose of the meeting was to discuss issues troubling blacks and to plan ways to gain equal rights. The Niagara Movement gave birth to the National Association for the Advancement of Colored People (NAACP). The NAACP was formed in 1909 by both black and white leaders. They wanted to work for black voting rights, for equal educational opportunities, and for an end to segregation. In 1910, other black leaders in New York City formed the Urban League. Its main goal was to help the large numbers of blacks who had come to live in the big cities of the North and Midwest. Both groups are still working today to improve the lives of black Americans.

Race Riots and Lynchings

Some whites reacted violently to black demands for fair treatment. During the years just before and after World War I, many whites joined the Ku Klux Klan, a "hate group" that was against blacks and other minorities. In addition, there were many lynchings in the South and Midwest. Blacks were hanged without trial, judge, or jury. At the end of World War I, race riots broke out all across the country. One of the worst riots started in Chicago on July 27, 1919. Twenty-three blacks and fifteen whites were killed. The NAACP and other black groups began a public campaign to end violence against blacks. The 20th-century civil rights movement had been born – and it would continue to work for the rights of black Americans. ∎

Either rent the video of the TV miniseries "Roots," or read Alex Haley's book of the same name. After you watch or read, think about ethnic pride. Why is it important for people to be proud of their group's past? How can people in the United States find out about their heritage? What ways of thinking might discourage people from finding out about it? How can people, especially immigrants, become "Americanized" without forgetting their roots?

Women's Rights

"**I**s woman making a man of herself?" asked one journalist in 1910. American women had been fighting for voting rights, known as *suffrage,* for more than 60 years. In a few states, women had gained their voting rights in the 1890s. But in the years between 1910 and 1920, it began to look as if women might finally win the national battle—and guarantee voting rights for all American women. Suffragettes across the country were marching in the streets, writing letters, handing out booklets, raising money, and pressuring politicians.

Why had the suffrage movement grown stronger during the war years? As men left to fight overseas, women had begun taking on jobs once given only to men. Ordinary American women decided that now was the time to act: "I didn't walk in New York's first suffrage parade, because my mother wouldn't let me," wrote one young woman. "Next year, in 1913, I wanted to march, but my husband asked me not to. This fall, I decided that it was 'up to me.'"

By the summer of 1920, the 19th Amendment to the Constitution, which would give voting rights to women, was almost a fact. It needed to be approved in only one more state. Women from all across the United States went to Knoxville, Tennessee, in

Jane Addams (right), social activist and reformer, in a women's suffrage parade. Addams also worked closely with immigrants to improve their lives.

August to watch a special meeting of the state legislature. It has been reported that as the lawmakers argued, the mother of the youngest member of the legislature called to her son from the balcony: "Hurrah! And vote for suffrage." His vote was "yes" – and it meant that the 19th Amendment had become law. ■

It is 1910. You are a suffragette. You are outraged that, in the 20th century, women do not have the vote in the United States. Write a letter about your feelings. It can be a public letter to a newspaper or a private letter to a family member.

Now it is 1920. The 19th Amendment has just been passed, and you have just voted for the first time. Write a diary entry telling how it felt to cast your first ballot.

THEN & NOW

After the battle for voting rights, many women of the 1920s worked for an equal rights amendment (ERA). They didn't get it. In the 1970s and 1980s, women tried – and failed – again.

Why did these two ERAs fail? In the 1920s, many people feared that an equal rights amendment would destroy laws that already protected women. They argued that laws guaranteeing child support, pensions, and other special protections would become illegal if the ERA said that women must be treated just like men. Many of the same arguments came up again during the ERA battles of the 1970s and 1980s. But since 1920, American women *have* won other equal-rights battles. Today's laws say women must get equal pay for their work and be given equal opportunities in education, sports, and other areas.

A Nation of Cities

"**H**ow you gonna keep 'em down on the farm/After they've seen Paree?" asked a song popular after World War I. The song was written about Americans who left their farms to fight in World War I. But it was about Americans at home too. During the war, many people left farms for "war work" jobs in the cities. Farmers from Kentucky and Illinois moved to cities to help build army trucks. Southern blacks went north to work in city factories that were making airplane engines and cars. New immigrants found work in city shipyards.

Immediately after the war ended, many "war work" jobs quickly disappeared. But the people stayed on in the cities. They had seen "Paree"— big cities such as Chicago, New York, Detroit, and Denver. After experiencing city life, they didn't want to go back to the farm.

As soldiers returned from Europe, America's cities grew even larger. City governments had trouble providing enough housing, plumbing, schools, and doctors for these newcomers. Cuts in factory jobs left many people out of work. And anti-immigration riots took place in cities across the United States. They were led by unemployed Americans who unjustly accused immigrants of taking jobs away from "real" Americans.

Life in the big city could be hard. So why did people stay? Many Americans stayed "in town" for the *fun* of it: for houses with electric lights and steam heat. For movie theaters and nightclubs. For new chain stores and

During and after World War I, many Americans moved to cities. This scene shows the bustling business district of Norwich, Connecticut.

A New Messiah?

"The business of America is business," said President Calvin Coolidge in 1925. For many Americans, a big part of the American Dream was "striking it rich" in business. Business leaders were admired. People looked up to them for advice on money, politics, and even religious issues. In fact, business became a kind of religion for many Americans. "Machinery is the new Messiah," said automaker Henry Ford. Many Americans began to believe that business and science, in place of religion, could solve the world's problems and make a "heaven on earth."

supermarkets. There were "dollars and cents" reasons to stay too. By 1920, crop prices were down, and it was hard to make money farming. Moreover, even though "war work" jobs were gone, new jobs were opening up in the cities, and some of them paid well. A city factory worker might earn enough to buy a Model T Ford – and have good city roads to drive it on!

During the 1920s and later, the number of Americans who lived and worked "down on the farm" got smaller every year. ■

"Buying on time" is perhaps even more popular today than it was in the 1920s. Many people believe that using credit cards allows them to buy more things. They believe that credit cards are convenient to use. Others believe that credit cards can cost you: fees and interest rates add to the cost of what you buy.

How do you feel about using credit cards? Are they convenient, or do they end up costing you more money?

Buy Now – Pay Later:
The Consumer Society Is Born

It's a Sunday evening in the mid-1920s. Sitting at the kitchen table, a young married couple is putting money in a stack of small envelopes. "That's $5 for the payment on the radio, $12 for the refrigerator, and $4 for the washing machine," says the husband. "And don't forget $15 for the new bedroom set," his wife adds.

Like many other Americans in the 1920s, this husband and wife have a houseful of items they're buying "on time." Instead of paying for things all at once, they make small payments every month. This was a new way of buying. How did it come about?

Business created "buying on time" to increase sales. American factories were producing more in the 1920s. American business needed consumers – buyers – for the sewing machines, cars, refrigerators, and gas cookers coming off the factory lines. But

these things were expensive. To help people afford them, business encouraged people to "buy now – pay later."

It was the right idea at the right time. For years, American inventors had been dreaming up new products. Manufacturers had found new and better ways to make those products. Then, in the 1920s, salaries went up. Prices went down. Americans wanted to use their new buying power to try the products they were seeing in advertisements. Here are just a few of the "toys" and household goods many Americans first tried after the war: cars, radios, and washing machines; vacuum cleaners and electric toasters; cellophane and cigarette lighters; wristwatches and canned food; Kleenex and zippers.

From 1909 to 1930, Sears, Roebuck and Co. sold houses by mail order. The house shown above arrived at its lot unassembled, with instructions.

Culture Shock

A popular song of the 1920s was "Anything Goes." The title meant that many new kinds of behavior were acceptable in the 1920s. They would have been considered "shocking" just a few years before. To many people of the time, the world seemed to be going mad. Ideas about right and wrong were changing quickly—especially among the young.

New Ideas about Dating

Once, "nice girls" *never* asked boys for dates; the male pursued the female. And dates were *not* a night out on the town. They usually took place at home, under the watchful eyes of parents. If young couples did go out, it was likely to be to a social—a get-together organized by their school or religious group. And a young couple never went out alone. A chaperon—an older family member or family friend—went with the couple to make sure that the two "behaved themselves."

By the 1920s, dating had changed. "Modern" young couples went out on dates—*alone.* It was no longer up to the male to ask the female out. Even "nice girls" asked boys out on dates. And while young couples might go to a social, they were just as likely to drive to a party, movie theater, or dance hall

in another town, where neighbors who knew them couldn't watch their every move. The automobile had given freedom and privacy to young people—and headaches to worried parents, who warned their daughters that an automobile was nothing but "a motel on wheels."

New Ideas about Sex

In the past, girls had been taught that sex was a wifely duty, something that women had to "put up with" to keep their husbands happy and to have children. Women weren't supposed to enjoy sex; they weren't even supposed to have sexual feelings. But by the 1920s, young women's views about sex were changing. They had begun to recognize their own sexuality and to think of sex as an important part of the bond between men and women.

Young women were being influenced by the work of psychoanalyst Sigmund Freud, whose ideas were sweeping America during the 1920s. Freud believed that sex was an important force in life and that people should become aware of their sexual feelings as a way to understand themselves. Freud's ideas helped to bring the subject of sex out in the open.

The Flapper

New ideas about sex were mirrored

by the way young women dressed. The "in" look for most of the decade was the flapper style – a freer, more openly "sexy" way of dressing than that favored by their grandmothers. Gone were long dresses, long sleeves, and thick cotton stockings worn by the older generation of women. In their place were short, sleeveless dresses (some with low-cut necklines) and silk stockings. To complete the look, young women wore face powder, rouge, and lipstick. Mothers and grandmothers were shocked, for when they were growing up, only "bad girls" wore makeup. Now, girls in the "best families" were wearing it. One mother in Muncie, Indiana, complained, "Girls aren't so modest nowadays. . . .We can't keep our boys decent." Another added, "Girls have more nerve nowadays – look at their clothes!"

Generation Gap

These mothers were not alone. Many in the older generation were upset by the behavior of young people. Grandparents and parents complained that young women didn't "know their place" and should "behave like ladies." In answer, one young woman wrote an open letter to the older generation that was published in the *North American Review* in 1925. She spoke for many young women of the time when she said, "You are letting me [do] work never before done by women. You are allowing me to be exposed . . . to conditions and temptations . . .women have never before been subjected to. . . . I am in factories, stores, and offices in the day time, and in theaters, at public dance halls . . . at night. . . . I am fending for myself in a world strange and alluring to me. I try all things, good and bad alike. You do not take responsibility for me. I will take it for myself."

Young men and women alike were questioning their parents' values and

Women's fashions in the 1920s (above). Police arrest people dressed in swimwear for "indecent exposure" in 1922 (below).

did not believe in the ideals of the Progressive Movement. They did not believe that good government could save the world. Many young men had fought in World War I. Many other young people had lost brothers or friends in the war. The government had not been able to stop the bloodiest fighting the world had ever seen. So, many young people asked, what good is it?

John F. Carter, Jr., summed up the feelings of many young people in an article he wrote for the *Atlantic Monthly* in 1920. He said, "The older generation pretty well ruined this world before passing it on to us. . . . Now my generation is disillusioned. . . .We have seen man at his lowest . . . in the terrible [war in Europe]. . . .We have seen the rottenness and shortcomings of all governments. . . . Into the past few years have been crowded the experiences and ideas of a . . . lifetime. . . .We have been forced to live in an atmosphere of 'tomorrow we die,' and so, naturally, we drank and were merry."

Churches and other religious groups joined the "older generation" in its fight against the younger generation's "dangerous" new attitudes. But their complaints fell on deaf ears. Fewer young people were attending religious services. Religion was no longer an important part of many of their lives. As the student editor of the Duke University *Chronicle* put it, "Someday [we] may settle down to the pew and the prayerbook, the prayer meeting and the Sunday sermon. But not now. Life is too sweet and too short . . . to waste it while [we are] still young." ■

This 1920s flapper demonstrates the Charleston, a popular dance of the period.

THEN & NOW

The "new" fashions of the 1920s were short, skinny, and slinky. As a result, many young women went on diets so that they could wear the "latest" styles. Newspapers and magazines of the time were filled with ads for diet aids, such as a special undergarment that supposedly could make "ugly pounds" disappear overnight. Some newspapers even began to include calorie counts with the recipes they published. And doctors of the time complained that young women were too worried about being thin. Sound familiar?

Fabulous Fads

With the passing of old values, the nation seemed to want to forget the "serious" issues of life. Crazy fads swept the nation. People wanted to be daring and different—as long as hundreds of other people were doing the same thing! Crossword puzzles, the card game bridge, and the Chinese table game mah-jongg became very popular. Both adults and children enjoyed roller-skating and yo-yos. There were contests of all kinds, from dance marathons (contests to see how long a couple could dance without resting) to flagpole sitting. In 1929, champion Alvin "Shipwreck" Kelly spent 145 days on flagpoles. Marathon dancer Mary "Hercules" Promitis made news by "pickling" her feet in vinegar and salt water. Why? To help her feet stand up to weeks of nonstop dancing. At the end of one three-week Madison Square Garden dance contest in 1928, Mary and her feet were feeling fine. ■

Flagpole sitting was one of many fads that swept the nation in the 1920s. Marathon dancing was another.

Troubled Times for the Family

In 1914, Mother's Day became a national holiday. But setting aside a day to honor mothers couldn't change the truth: Americans were afraid that family life was in trouble.

For one thing, divorce was on the rise. In 1914, there were about 100,000 divorces in the United States. In 1929, there were 205,000. Another problem: family members were spending more time apart from each other. In the past, families had worked a farm or run a store together. Many children had been educated at home too. But by the 1920s, Dad was away at the office, shop, or factory. Older children were in

Don't Touch the Baby!
Child Care: New World and Old

"Never hug and kiss them, never let them sit in your lap." That was the advice of John B. Watson, a famous American psychologist in the early 1900s. His advice on how to raise children surprised many immigrants. In the old country, most families had never read a book about child care. They had fed and hugged their children whenever the time seemed right. Immigrant grandmothers thought their daughters were silly to read about raising children. But young immigrant mothers wanted to do things the American way. One mother remembers:

"Everything had to be on schedule. I took the book with me everywhere. . . .When the kids went to bed, no one, but no one, not even God Himself, was allowed to disturb them. My in-laws . . . thought I was crazy." Another woman remembers trying to keep her own mother from comforting the sobbing baby at a "wrong" time. "She just pushed me away and went in and picked up the baby," the woman said. Another mother found that because she seldom touched the baby, she hadn't noticed an infected birthmark. This birthmark had been making the baby cry: "After that I said, 'To hell with the book.'"

Twenty years later, child-care experts would change their minds again. By the 1940s, most of them agreed that the old country ways of showing affection to children were better after all.

school. Mom was at home with the youngest children. If money was a problem, she held a job outside the home.

People found plenty of blame to spread around. They said the family was breaking down because too many women wanted to smoke, vote, cut their hair, and wear pants like men. They blamed working women who would not stay home. They also blamed birth control. More couples were using it to keep their family small. Many Americans thought these changes meant that the family might disappear. Others said change might make family life *better*. ■

People thought the family was in trouble in the 1920s. Some people think it is in trouble today. They point to some of the same evidence: rising divorce rates, shrinking birthrates, a values gap between parents and children.

Do you think the family is in trouble these days? What evidence do you see that makes you think it is or isn't? What forces in society do you think are pulling the family apart? What can be done to strengthen the family?

The Age of Vaudeville

Where did America go for a good time? In the early years of the century, *fun* meant a vaudeville show. Vaudeville had a little of everything: talking dogs, opera singers, comics, jugglers, acrobats, the latest songs and dances . . . and more! Audiences were treated to a variety of acts in shows that changed from week to week. One week, the star act might be a pair of tap-dancing twins. The next week, it might be an actor doing a scene from a Shakespeare play. Because shows changed often, vaudeville entertainers did not stay in one place for very long. They traveled from theater to theater, doing their acts in one city one week and another city the next. They lived on trains and in hotel rooms, and they

George Burns is shown in his 20s (left) with his wife and vaudeville partner, Gracie Allen, and (right) in his 90s. After vaudeville, Burns found new careers in radio, television, and movies.

seldom saw their families – unless their families were part of the act.

Most small towns had at least one vaudeville theater. Big cities had several. George Burns, who was a vaudeville star, recalls: "There were so many theaters . . . that if a performer had fourteen good minutes [of material] he could work six years without changing a word or playing the same theater twice." But if audiences saw the same act twice, they didn't mind. Vaudeville performers were like old friends who had come for a visit.

Vaudeville performers worked hard. They did three shows a day and five on Saturday and Sunday. Small-time vaudeville performers dreamed of playing the Palace Theater in New York

City. They worked hard to "make it." Judy Garland had been an international movie and singing star for many years when she finally played the Palace in 1951. "It's like finally reaching the promised land," she said.

Vaudeville shows were a true "melting pot" of people with different backgrounds and talents. Outside the theater, there might be tension between groups. But on the vaudeville stage, a Russian Jewish immigrant could sing songs written by a German immigrant or put on dark makeup to sing a "Negro" spiritual. Jokes about different ethnic groups were a regular part of the vaudeville routine – and the laughter was good-humored.

But while vaudeville used the talents of many recent European immigrants, black Americans found the going harder. Some black acts reached star status and even played the Palace. But many blacks could perform only in all-black shows. And in many vaudeville theaters, black performers were not welcome at all. ■

W. C. Fields (left) is shown here when he was a vaudeville tramp juggler. He later became famous in comedy films. An advertisement (below) for "polite" vaudeville.

Vol. V.

Washington, D. C., Week of October 6, 1902.

No. 5.

CHASE'S

P. B. CHASE, proprietor-
H. WINNIFRED DE WITT, manager-

DEVOTED TO
MR. CHASE'S ORIGINAL IDEA
POLITE VAUDEVILLE

IN THE PRESENTATION OF POLITE VAUDEVILLE IN THE CHASE THEATRES IT IS THE CONSTANT AIM OF THE MANAGEMENT TO PREVENT THE USE OF A SINGLE WORD, EXPRESSION, OR SITUATION THAT WILL OFFEND THE INTELLIGENT, REFINED AND CULTURED CLASSES.

NOW PLAYING:
America and the Movies

In the late 1800s, Americans laughed and cried over the stories they read in magazines and books. But in the early 1900s, movies became the biggest storyteller.

At first, movies were shown on "nickelodeon" machines. To see a movie, a person put a nickel in the machine, and it showed a moving picture. These early movies were only a minute or two long—and there was no sound.

Gradually, movies became more like the movies we know today. *The Great Train Robbery* (1903) was only 12 minutes long—but it was the first movie that told a complete story with a beginning, middle, and end. During the 1920s, movies began to tell longer stories with more complicated plots. And the movies weren't silent anymore. Al Jolson's 1927 movie *The Jazz Singer* introduced "talkies"—movies with sound. Movies were advertised as "all-talking, all-singing," and more Americans than ever went to the movies. By the end of the 1920s, millions of Americans were going to the movies every week.

A scene from the 1903 movie *The Great Train Robbery* (below left). A poster for *The Jazz Singer* (below right), the very first "talkie"—a movie with sound.

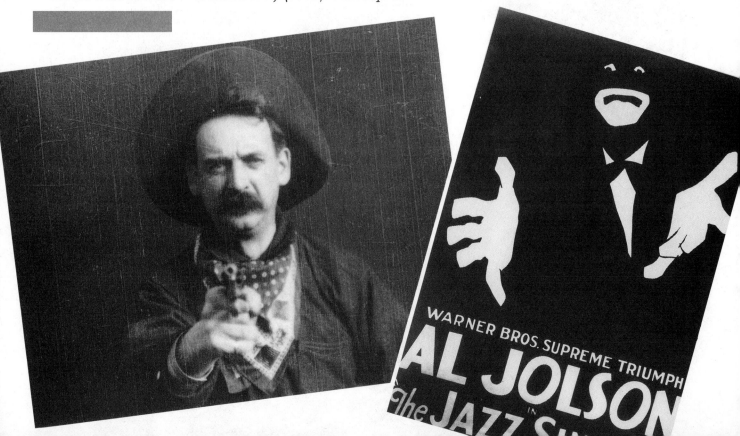

WARNER BROS. SUPREME TRIUMPH
AL JOLSON
IN
The JAZZ SIN

Movies showed how much America was changing in the new century. They showed the new styles and fashions to Americans all over the country. They showed the latest inventions: cars, telephones, airplanes, phonograph records. And movies introduced America's middle class to new and different lifestyles, manners, and morals. Like giant factories, Hollywood studios turned out movie "dreams" of the good life in America. Many Americans tried to live up to those movie dreams—by dressing and acting like the people on the movie screen.

Movie stars were the newest American heroes. Audiences laughed at the comedies of Charlie Chaplin, Harold Lloyd, and Buster Keaton. They were thrilled when Douglas Fairbanks played a dashing pirate sailing the seven seas. They loved the innocence of Mary Pickford and the beauty of Greta Garbo. And they worshiped romantic star Rudolph Valentino. When he died in 1926, more than 30,000 fans came to his funeral. The large crowd nearly caused a riot.

Charlie Chaplin and the American Dream

No movie character of the 1920s was loved more than Charlie Chaplin's "Little Tramp." What was it people loved about this childlike character? Like plenty of other people, the Tramp seemed a bit confused by modern machines and technology. And in a time when many Americans seemed too worried about money and success, Chaplin's Tramp reminded people of a simpler, friendlier time.

Many movie critics believe that Chaplin's 1925 film *The Gold Rush* shows Chaplin's feelings about the runaway greed of the 1920s. In this movie, the Little Tramp turns up in the Alaskan gold rush of the 1890s. He is among men and women who care only about gold—and the things gold can buy. The Tramp loses his girl and his best friend to the gold fever. But he never loses his belief that people are more important than money.

Chaplin was a comedy genius. But so were other silent movie clowns of that time. What did moviegoers love about the Little Tramp? Maybe it was his ability to find love and warmth—even in the clutter and noise and greed of modern life.

Silent film stars: Rudolph Valentino (above left) is best remembered as *The Sheik*. Comedy legend Charlie Chaplin (above right) is shown here in his familiar tramp character.

Sultry movie stars Clara Bow (above left) and Theda Bara (above right) show the "modern" attitudes of the 1920s. Clara Bow was known as the "It" girl — meaning that she had sex appeal. By 1930, the film industry had set up a production code in order to make movies "moral."

Sex on the Screen

During the 1920s, sex began to play a larger role in movies. In fact, movies had so much sex in them that many people were shocked.

The new "sexiness" of movies changed the kinds of roles women played on screen. In movies made shortly after 1900, women usually played sweethearts, wives, sisters, and mothers. But by the 1920s, new images of women were pouring onto the screen: the jazz-loving "flapper," the independent career girl, the woman of adventure and daring.

Star Clara Bow was everybody's idea of the "flapper," the modern girl with modern ideas — especially about love and sexuality. She was called the "It" girl. In those days, having "It" meant you had sex appeal.

By 1930, the film industry was worried that things had gone too far. It set up the first production code. The purpose of the code was to control the morality of the movies. The code set up stricter rules. Women's costumes had to be more modest. Movies could not show a husband and wife sharing the same bed. And the "bad guys" had to be punished by the end of the movie. Not until the 1970s and 1980s were the movies as bold as they had been during the 1920s. ■

Rent a movie comedy of the 1920s. As you watch it, compare what people thought was funny then with what they find funny now. How does the old movie show women, racial minorities, and so on? Would images of these groups from the 1920s be acceptable today?

Rent and watch Charlie Chaplin's The Gold Rush. *How does Chaplin's character win the affection of viewers? How is the Little Tramp a comment on the American Dream of money and security?*

Voices in the Air

In the 1920s, radio broadcasts began to compete with the movies for America's free time. The first regular radio broadcasts came in 1920 from station KDKA in Pittsburgh. The station carried news, church services, and some music. By 1929, more than 600 radio stations were on the air in the United States. That year, Americans spent an estimated $850 million to buy radios and spare parts.

American families gathered around the radio to hear favorite shows, much as families today watch TV together. "Until radio came along," remembers George Burns, "home entertainment [was] listening to a relative play the piano or violin, dropping a stray cat on top of the sleeping pet dog, or slipping a whoopee cushion under the old man's chair." But with a radio in the house, families didn't have to wait for once-a-year visits from favorite vaudeville acts or tent shows. The "big show" was on the air every night of the year – to be enjoyed by all.

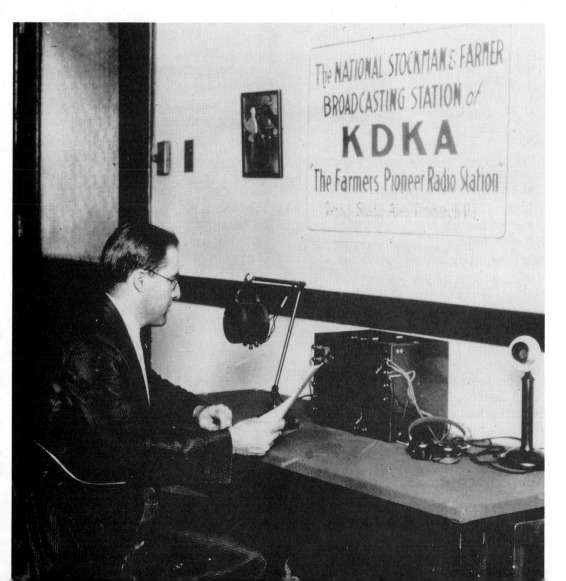

Early broadcast studios looked like this almost bare room in East Liberty, Pennsylvania. KDKA was the first regularly transmitting radio station in the world. Just nine years after it began regular broadcasts, over 600 radio stations were on the air.

25 Cents
February
1924
Over 200 Illustrations

RADIO NEWS

REG. U.S. PAT. OFF.

Edited by H. GERNSBACK

"CRACK IT WITH MUSIC!"

IN THIS ISSUE
THE ULTRADYNE
CIRCUIT
BY R. E. LACAULT
See Page
1058

THE 100% WIRELESS MAGAZINE

Radio helped unite Americans. Its growing popularity is shown by this cover of a 1924 issue of *Radio News*.

THEN & NOW

By the end of the 1920s, commercials were a regular part of the radio scene. Airtime was a bargain, too. A sponsor could buy all the advertising time on a one-hour NBC radio show for about $10,000. In contrast, just *30 seconds* of commercial time on a prime-time NBC television show today costs about $160,000.

Not everyone was happy with the marriage of radio and advertising. Dr. Lee De Forest, who invented the vacuum tube and helped make broadcast radio possible, was particularly unhappy. He asked, "What have you done to my child? You have sent him out on the street [like a singing beggar] . . . to collect money from all."

Radio Unites the Country

Radio connected Americans in a new way. From coast to coast, people listened to the same news and opinions. They laughed at "Amos 'n' Andy," a show about black people in Harlem. They danced to the music of the Paul Whiteman orchestra. And they listened to the same radio ads for coffee, soap, refrigerators, and other products.

Radio listeners were united by real-life drama too. They heard news reports about ongoing events, and they wondered how the story would end. Would young pilot Charles Lindbergh make it all the way to Paris on the first solo nonstop flight across the Atlantic? (Yes.) Could boxer Jack Dempsey come back to defeat the younger champion, Gene Tunney? (No.) Would a Tennessee jury convict a young teacher for teaching the theory of evolution? (Yes, but he didn't go to jail.) The radio brought famous people and faraway places right into our living rooms. Almost overnight, radio made the world seem to be a smaller place. ■

How is modern radio different from what was on KDKA radio? Think of the different kinds of programs that can be heard across your radio dial today.

Take a product that you use and like, and write a radio ad for it. Remember: you cannot show the product; you have to describe it with words alone.

America on Paper: Writers and Poets

Most American literature before World War I was optimistic and hopeful. Like the rest of the world, most writers believed in the 19th-century idea of progress. They felt the world was getting better every year. Poets such as Robert Frost and Amy Lowell wrote about the quiet beauty of everyday life. Writers praised the energy and strength of American cities. The years before World War I were, as critic Van Wyck Brooks put it, "confident years."

World War I changed everyone's life. It changed the literary world too. Many young writers and poets fought in the war, and some died in it. Those who lived had seen a new kind of war. This was a war in which millions died, in which homes were bombed and families killed, in which chemical weapons were first used. Writers began to talk about the world as an evil and empty place – a world where nothing ever really changed for the better. It was a world, said British poet Wilfred Owen, where young men were sent to fight for "the old lie" about honor and glory. American poet Ezra Pound said millions of people had died for a world that was like an old toothless dog – not worth saving.

During and after the war, some writers left the United States for new lives in Europe. Among these writers were novelist Ernest Hemingway and poet T. S. Eliot. Hemingway's stories tell of men and women living restless, empty lives. His characters reject the values of the past – but they have not

Ernest Hemingway (above) and T. S. Eliot (below) were two of America's most influential writers. Hemingway's stories tell about the "Lost Generation" – modern men and women who live restless lives, cut off from the values of the past. Eliot's poetry portrays the modern world as a "waste land."

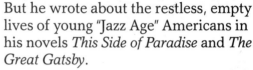

Writer F. Scott Fitzgerald and family in 1925 (above), the year _The Great Gatsby_, his most famous novel, was published. A dapper Sinclair Lewis (below), the first American to win the Nobel Prize for literature.

found anything to replace them with. T. S. Eliot wrote of the world as a ruined "waste land" where "hollow men" wait for the world to end "not with a bang but a whimper."

Critics of the American Dream

Whether American writers lived in Europe or stayed at home, they often wrote about the new, fast-paced America of the 1920s. Novelist F. Scott Fitzgerald spent much time in Paris.

But he wrote about the restless, empty lives of young "Jazz Age" Americans in his novels _This Side of Paradise_ and _The Great Gatsby_.

Many American writers criticized the America they saw around them in the 1920s. In his novels _Main Street_ and _Babbitt_, novelist Sinclair Lewis wrote about an America that was "all business"—more interested in making money than in meeting people's needs. The name Babbitt became a term used to describe a certain kind of American middle-class businessman: one who is narrow-minded, conservative, satisfied that his ideas are always right. Rising playwright Eugene O'Neill also criticized America and its attitude toward business in _The Great God Brown_. Newspaperman H. L. Mencken made fun of American business too—and just about everything else in the country.

Many critics believe that the years after World War I produced more great American literature than any other time. Writers, poets, and playwrights were rebelling against the America of yesterday. That rebellion gave them new freedom—freedom to write in new ways, and freedom to see the world with new eyes. ∎

Look for more fiction or poetry by writers mentioned in "America on Paper." Ernest Hemingway, in particular, wrote simply and clearly but with great emotional truth. Some Hemingway stories to consider: "Indian Camp," "The Doctor and the Doctor's Wife," "The End of Something," and "A Clean, Well-Lighted Place."

Black and Beautiful

In the 1920s, the New York City neighborhood of Harlem became a center of black American life and culture. Sometimes it seemed that the whole world was on its way to Harlem. Young black writers from all across the United States came to talk and to write. Their stories were published in the new black literary magazines. Jazz musicians, dancers, and singers took the train north from New Orleans or Memphis. White novelists and composers came to hear the rhythms of black speech and music. And rich New Yorkers dressed up to visit Harlem night spots like the famous Cotton Club.

The Harlem Renaissance

It was all a part of what is today called the "Harlem Renaissance"—an outpouring of creativity from black writers, poets, composers, and performers of the 1920s. When Americans think of "black pride" today, they think of the civil rights movement of the 1960s and beyond. But another kind of pride grew in the Harlem of the 1920s.

Music, especially jazz, was an important part of Harlem's creative life. Jazz was the theme music of the 1920s. Black performers Louis Armstrong and Duke Ellington played jazz in the Harlem nightclubs; white

Louis Armstrong (left) was a great jazz musician who rose to fame in the 1920s. He and other jazz legends such as Duke Ellington (below, with the Washingtonians) played their music in Harlem nightclubs during the 1920s.

readers only what I would be proud for them to see? Writers found different answers. Countee Cullen and Claude McKay wrote powerful poems about black life and emotions—but they used the language and forms of "white" poetry. Poet Langston Hughes went in another direction. He used black speech patterns and "blues" rhythms in his poetry. To some, Hughes's poems seemed closer to the real experience of black Americans:

> I was a red man one time.
> But the white men came.
> I was a black man, too.
> But the white men came.
> They drove me out of the forest.
> They took me away from the jungles.
> I lost my trees.
> I lost my silver moons.
> Now they've caged me
> In the circus of civilization.
> Now I herd with the many—
> Caged in the circus of civilization.
> -"Lament for Dark Peoples"

"Why is it important for us to know of . . . the men and women of the Harlem Renaissance?" black novelist John Oliver Killens once asked. Many young black Americans, he said, believe that the black liberation movement began in the 1960s. But there was plenty of "black pride" in 1920s Harlem too. "We need desperately to know that this generation is not the first to produce artists and writers . . . who identified with Africa and proclaimed that Black was beautiful." ■

Langston Hughes (above left) used the rhythms of jazz and the patterns of black speech to create a new style of poetry. Bessie Smith (above right), the "Empress of the Blues," sold millions of records in the 1920s.

composer George Gershwin played it at Carnegie Hall. Jazz became a link between black America and white America. While their parents might go to Harlem to hear jazz, American teenagers danced to jazz tunes played by white orchestras.

Writers and Questions

Up the stairs or around the corner from the jazz clubs, young black writers were meeting together and asking important questions: Should I write like whites, or should I draw from black folklore and speech patterns? Should I write honestly about black life, or should I show white

Check libraries for recordings by musicians who were part of or influenced by the Harlem Renaissance. You should be able to find Louis Armstrong, Duke Ellington, Bessie Smith, and Fats Waller music there.

Newcomers

The years after World War I were good times for newspapers and magazines. Americans had developed an appetite for news during the war. People had more free time for reading, and more adults *could* read. There was something for everyone. Children and grown-ups often turned first to the "funnies"—pages full of popular comic strips like "Buster Brown," "Mutt and Jeff," and "The Katzenjammer Kids." Tabloid newspapers gained millions of new readers with sensational stories of sex and violence. And in the mid-1920s, three important magazines came out for the first time: *Reader's Digest, Time,* and *The New Yorker.* They were very different from one another.

The *Reader's Digest* reprinted articles from other magazines and books. Its articles were full of optimism. The magazine supported conservative political views and told Americans to live moral lives and help themselves become successful. The *Digest* was aimed at middle-class and working-class readers. It was a little monthly package of useful and entertaining writing.

Time magazine was a kind of

A city newsstand in the 1920s — where people could buy magazines such as *Time,* the *Reader's Digest,* and *The New Yorker.*

THE READER'S DIGEST

THIRTY-ONE ARTICLES EACH MONTH FROM LEADING MAGAZINES — EACH ARTICLE OF ENDURING VALUE AND INTEREST, IN CONDENSED AND COMPACT FORM

FEBRUARY 1922

Since it began in 1925, *The New Yorker* has featured "Eustace Tilley" on the cover of its anniversary issues each year. The *Reader's Digest* had shortened versions of articles from other magazines.

"reader's digest" too. It fed people's desire to be informed – without having to work too hard at it. Henry Luce, who started *Time*, said he was interested in "slicing, trimming, flavoring, coloring, and packaging" the news of the day. *Time* writers of the 1920s didn't gather and report the news themselves. They read dozens of daily newspapers. Then they rewrote the news using the methods of fiction writers. *Time* articles were "short stories" with beginnings, middles, and endings.

The New Yorker magazine bragged that it was "not for the little old lady in Dubuque." It wanted readers who were educated, "citified," and politically liberal. *The New Yorker* made fun of the older, middle-class values of some Americans – the kind of people who would read the *Reader's Digest*. The magazine was a home for the latest fiction from America's finest writers, including James Thurber, Robert Benchley, and Dorothy Parker. *The New Yorker*, said the magazine's loyal fans, was truly witty. Others said it was *too* clever, too quick to make fun of ordinary people.

All three magazines still exist today. But are they the same as they were in the 1920s? Pick up a copy of each at the library – and see what *you* think. ■

While you are at the library, look at current issues of Time, *the* Reader's Digest, *and* The New Yorker. *Magazines do change – are these three still much the same as "Newcomers" describes them?*

Shakespeare in Yiddish?

In the years after 1900, many immigrant groups developed their own theaters. It was fun—and comforting—to hear songs or see plays from the "old country." The theater was one way to keep customs alive in a new land.

The liveliest theater scene of all was the Jewish theater of New York City. It is usually called "Yiddish" theater because plays and songs were performed in Yiddish. Yiddish is a mixture of German, Hebrew, Aramaic, French, Italian, and other languages. It has been used for centuries by European Jews.

During World War I, there were 20 Yiddish theaters in New York City, plus Yiddish music halls, vaudeville theaters, and rooftop cabarets. Playwright Sholom Aleichem turned his stories into plays for the Yiddish theater. His most famous play was *Tevye the Dairyman*. In the 1960s, it was retold in English as *Fiddler on the Roof*.

In the Yiddish theater, audiences saw translated plays of Shakespeare and Norwegian playwright Henrik Ibsen. They saw Yiddish versions of current American stage "hits" and original plays about immigrant life in the new land. Plays from Europe were often performed in the Yiddish theater years before they appeared anywhere else in New York City. ∎

This poster is a 1919 advertisement for a Yiddish translation of a play by Russian writer Maxim Gorki.

Athletes: Our National Heroes

After losing the heavyweight title to Gene Tunney (right) a year earlier, Jack Dempsey (left) tries to regain the crown in this 1927 fight. The controversial fight became known as the battle of the "Long Count."

During the 1920s, a war-weary public was looking for relief from the stress and strain of American life. A major source of entertainment was the sporting events that radio brought into America's living rooms. Also during the 1920s, newspapers started to take athletic events seriously. They covered the contests and their players, using the colorful language that is still the stamp of sports writing. As a result of this attention, Americans began a love affair with sports that continues today.

As early as the 1920s, Americans began to look up to gifted athletes as national heroes. At boxing arenas, baseball parks, and football stadiums,

fans were eager to pay money to see these new gladiators of the 20th century.

If any sport is closely connected with the 1920s, it would have to be boxing. During that period, this sport became highly popular with the American public. Promoter Tex Rickard had a great deal to do with this popularity. He is known for producing boxing's first million-dollar gate (ticket receipts of a million dollars).

Boxing in all weight categories was popular. However, the heavyweight

class dominated all others. It was in 1920, as well, that the National Boxing Association (later to become the World Boxing Association) was founded.

The Dempsey Years

Few athletes dominate a sport as handily as boxer Jack Dempsey did in his day. He held the heavyweight boxing title from July 1919 to September 1926. The most celebrated boxer of his time, Dempsey brought in the first million-dollar gate in boxing history. At this fight, more than 80,000 fans saw him defeat the French war hero Georges Carpentier.

In 1926, Dempsey fought newcomer Gene Tunney in Philadelphia. Tunney shocked boxing fans by beating Dempsey. The next year, a rematch was held in Chicago. This time, more than 100,000 fans paid more than $2 million to watch the most talked-about fight in boxing history.

Dempsey knocked down Tunney in the seventh round. But Dempsey stood over his opponent instead of going to a neutral corner of the ring. Tunney got up before the count of 10 and went on to win the bout. Dempsey did not regain the crown. The fight became known as the battle of the "Long Count."

The Great White Hope

Preceding Dempsey in popularity was Jack Johnson. He won the heavyweight title in 1908, but his long career spanned the 1920s. Johnson was a hero to black Americans at a time when blacks could not freely participate in national sports.

Johnson was born in Galveston, Texas, into a family that could trace its African roots. The son of a former slave, he started boxing in exhibitions at $5 a show. By the time he was 30, he had beaten all the black fighters. He wanted a chance to box for the world

heavyweight crown.

In those days, white fighters avoided being matched with blacks. But Johnson was determined. He followed the champion, Canadian Tommy Burns, to Australia. After many challenges, Burns finally agreed to fight Johnson. The match was held in Sydney.

In the ring, Johnson made fun of Burns while landing punch after punch. Some white watchers, including writer Jack London, wanted to see the smile wiped from Johnson's face. Local police had to stop the fight in the 14th round, and Johnson was awarded the KO.

Many Americans hated the idea of a black champion and looked for the

In 1908, Jack Johnson became the first black heavyweight champion by knocking out Tommy Burns.

Babe Ruth, the "Sultan of Swat," is one of the most famous athletes of all time. His 714 career home runs stood as a record for many years.

"Great White Hope"—a white man to defeat Johnson. But Johnson beat white challengers Stanley Ketchel in 1909 and Jim Jeffries in 1910. Jeffries was the undefeated former champ who was called out of retirement to face Johnson. The 1910 fight set off race riots and lynchings across the country.

Besides envying Johnson for his great boxing ability, many Americans disliked him for driving expensive cars and wearing flashy clothes. Moreover, three of Johnson's four wives were white.

Johnson was found guilty of violating the Mann Act, a law that forbade taking females across state lines for "immoral purposes." To escape a prison sentence, Johnson fled to Canada, disguised as a baseball player, and then to Europe. In 1915, a fight was arranged for him in Havana, Cuba.

In this fight, Johnson lost the crown to Jess Willard, a farmer from Kansas. Willard knocked him out in the 26th round, but Johnson maintained to his death that the fight was fixed. Because of his earlier conviction, Johnson was sent to jail after he returned to the United States.

The Sultan of Swat: Babe Ruth

At about the same time that Jack Dempsey was dominating the sport of boxing, Babe Ruth was establishing himself as the outstanding baseball player of the time.

Even today, he is probably the greatest of all sports heroes. George Herman Ruth, better known as Babe Ruth, remains firmly stamped in the history of baseball, America's national pastime.

Ruth spent much of his youth in a Baltimore orphanage/reform school. As an adult, he was known for his genuine love for children and his great appetite for food, drink, and—some said—women. Ruth stood 6 feet 2 inches tall and, in his prime, weighed 215 pounds.

Ruth could hit as well as pitch. Though he pitched in 17 games in 1919, that year marked Ruth's first full season playing primarily as an outfielder. His 29 home runs in 1919 broke the major-league record.

In 1920, the Boston Red Sox sold Ruth to the New York Yankees, the team he is chiefly associated with in baseball fans' minds. Playing for the Yanks, Babe shattered his own home run record by hitting 54 home runs in 1920 and 59 in 1921. He reached his highest home run total, 60, in 1927. The Yankees won the American League title that year and five other times in the 1920s. In 1930, Ruth earned $80,000—more than the president of the United States. When he was asked to defend his record salary, he said, "Why not? I had a better year. . . ."

Baseball's Biggest Scandal

Legend has it that a boy approached baseball star Joe Jackson outside a Chicago courtroom. "Say it ain't so, Joe," he said. Jackson responded, "Son, I'm afraid it is." These few words sum up baseball's biggest scandal.

Baseball star Joe Jackson and seven of his teammates were accused of taking money to lose the 1919 World Series.

The World Series was already a big event by 1910. Then, as now, it determined the best team in baseball. The Cincinnati Reds won the 1919 series over the Chicago White Sox, five games to three. But after the series was over, there were rumors that White Sox players had been bribed by gamblers to lose.

According to informers, gamblers from New York worked through a White Sox first baseman, Chick Gandil. He was accused of persuading the seven other players to let the Reds win.

Over the next winter, baseball team owners hired a judge to become baseball's "commissioner." His name was Kenesaw Mountain Landis, and his main job was to investigate the rumors.

Comiskey Park, home of the Chicago White Sox from 1910 through 1990. Eight White Sox players were accused of taking money to lose the 1919 World Series.

Landis carefully interviewed the players suspected of wrongdoing. A court trial was held. After the trial, all eight players were found innocent. Many people thought the players had "gotten off" through the efforts of smart lawyers. This protected the gamblers who had planned the fix. No gamblers were ever brought to trial. Despite the "not guilty" verdict, Judge Landis banned all eight players from baseball for the rest of their lives.

In recent years, much of the interest in the "Black Sox" scandal has focused on Joe Jackson. He was a great player, and the game of baseball lost a lot when he was banned. During the trial, he said he turned down Gandil's offer to cheat. For years, both before and since his death in 1951, people have made efforts to have his name cleared. But neither Commissioner Landis nor later commissioners have cleared him of the charges.

We may never know all there is to know about the infamous Black Sox scandal. But it still affects the game. When baseball's Pete Rose was banned from the game in 1989 for gambling, events of 70 years before were on everyone's mind. ∎

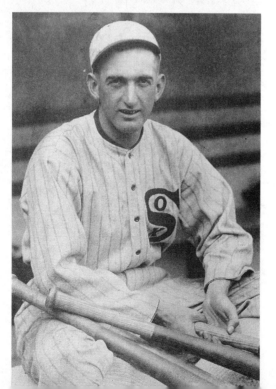

The "Black Sox" with their attorneys (above) in 1921. Star player Joe Jackson is second from the left. Jackson (right) in uniform.

Babe Ruth made more money than President Hoover in 1930. Today, the average baseball player's salary is much higher than President Bush's pay. Athletes in other sports are also very highly paid. It's true that pro athletes bring in a lot of money for team owners. But do you think that they are worth what they are paid? In your opinion, what kinds of workers should make more money than pro athletes make? How do you feel about the fact, for instance, that a good teacher may not make 1/20 the salary of a good shortstop? What does this say—if anything—about our society's focus on sports?

Two excellent movies about the "Black Sox" scandal have come out in recent years. Eight Men Out *tells the story in a realistic way;* Field of Dreams *is a fantasy about the Black Sox. Both should be available to rent at video stores. View them, and see how they make you feel about "Shoeless Joe" Jackson and the "Black Sox."*

The Birth of the
N·F·L

These factory workers played football games on weekends. Two years after this photo was taken, the Decatur Staleys became the Chicago Bears. Coach/player George Halas is in the middle of the front row.

On September 17, 1920, a group of team owners met in Canton, Ohio, to organize a professional football league. Each was supposed to have paid $100 to join the new league. Most of the men there came from small cities near the Great Lakes: Akron, Canton, Cleveland, and Dayton (Ohio); Hammond and Muncie (Indiana); Rochester (New York); and Decatur, Chicago, and Rock Island (Illinois).

Olympic great Jim Thorpe was selected as president but had no role in the formation of the league. He was chosen because he was famous and had been a star player. His term was only one year.

One member of the new league was the Decatur Staleys. The team was named after its sponsor, the A. E. Staley Company. The Staleys' man at Canton was former University of Illinois player George Halas.

As the Staleys' coach, Halas faced a challenge: finding enough football players willing to play for a few dollars on weekends—and make cornstarch on weekdays. The company allowed them to practice two hours a day on company time.

By 1922, Halas had moved his team to Chicago and renamed it the Bears. The league also changed its original name from the American Professional Football Association (APFA) to the National Football League. At first it struggled, but gradually it grew more popular and expanded its franchises. To sell people on football, teams traveled across the country playing exhibition games.

In 1925, Tim Mara bought a franchise for New York City – the Giants. By that time, major-league teams had been established not only in Chicago, but also in Cleveland, Buffalo, Milwaukee, Minneapolis, and Louisville.

Halas caused a sensation when he signed "Red" Grange to a pro contract after the 1925 college season. Grange,

Jim Thorpe: All-American

One of the great American Olympic heroes was Jim Thorpe. During the 1912 games, Thorpe, an American Indian, gained worldwide fame. He won the decathlon (10 events, including running, hurdling, jumping, and throwing) and the pentathlon (five events) at Stockholm, Sweden. The king of Sweden said Thorpe was "the greatest athlete in the world."

Before he played in the Olympics, Thorpe had been an All-American football player at the Carlisle Indian School in Pennsylvania. His skills made the school famous. After his accomplishments in Sweden, Americans greeted him with a hero's welcome.

Then it was discovered that he had played semipro baseball for a few dollars during vacations from college before competing in the Olympics. He did not know that it would endanger his amateur status, a requirement for playing in the Olympics. He had not played in professional sports but was stripped of his Olympic medals anyway.

Humiliated, Thorpe fought to have his medals restored. But stubborn Olympic officials refused to back down. The medals finally were restored in 1982 – long after Thorpe had died.

It would be hard to find a modern-day equal to Jim Thorpe. Though several modern athletes have excelled in two major sports (Bo Jackson of football and baseball being the most recent example), to compare with Jim Thorpe, an athlete would also have to high-jump, pole-vault, shot-put, sprint, and run long distances. Moreover, he would have to play pro baseball and football and also be good at basketball, boxing, lacrosse, and swimming. It is said that there were only three sports that Thorpe *didn't* play: cricket, croquet, and golf. Since 1955, the NFL's most valuable player award has been called the Jim Thorpe Trophy.

Jim Thorpe is considered by many to be the greatest athlete of all time. He was stripped of his Olympic gold medals because he had played baseball for money before competing in the Olympic games.

who played for the University of Illinois, was football's first dazzling runner. In a 1924 game against the University of Michigan, Grange ran back the opening kickoff 95 yards for a touchdown. Before the end of the first quarter, he had made touchdown runs of 67, 56, and 44 yards. Halas immediately took his team on a cross-country tour of 18 exhibition games – including eight in a 12-day stretch. Huge crowds – including 73,000 in New York City – saw games in large cities. Professional football was on its way. ■

The article says pro football's Super Bowl is a "kind of midwinter national holiday in the United States." Ask a number of people you know whether they think this is true. Ask them how important the Super Bowl is to them. Write a paragraph summing up the results of your research.

Football legend "Red" Grange breaks away from tacklers in a University of Illinois game. The "Galloping Ghost" once scored four touchdowns in a single quarter.

THEN & NOW

Football in the 1920s had the same basic rules as today. It was played using the same strategies – although different offenses and defenses are always being tried.

But the game *looked* very different. In the past, it was played on grass in run-down stadiums. Now it often is played on artificial turf in such sports palaces as the New Orleans Superdome and the Indianapolis Hoosier Dome.

In earlier days, players wore soft leather helmets, if they wore them at all. Padding often was no thicker than cardboard. There was no face protection. Few pro players ended up with all their teeth. Today, hard helmets, face guards, and mouthpieces protect the head, face, and teeth. And teams now use specialists in athletic injuries to treat the players.

Teams in the 1920s used to hope that some local reporters would come to see their games. Today, billion-dollar contracts with TV networks bring football to the nation and to the world. The Super Bowl, pro football's championship game, is a kind of midwinter national holiday in the United States.

Athletes in Other Sports

By the 1920s, women athletes had started to become famous. They first gained attention in the sport of tennis. The biggest star, Suzanne Lenglen of France, won a world championship at age 15 in 1914. She won at Wimbledon in 1919 and five more times in the 1920s. She was known for her graceful, careful strategy. She also changed the way women tennis players dressed: She caused a stir when she showed up at Wimbledon in a calf-length, short-sleeved dress.

Helen Wills was called the "Queen of the Nets." She dominated tennis from 1923 to the mid-1930s. At the time, many players talked to crowds and boasted to the press. Wills did not. "When I play, I become entirely absorbed in the game," she said. For this reason, she was also known as "Little Miss Poker Face." The nickname came from her seriousness and her cool, efficient game. She was U.S. singles champ seven times between 1923 and 1931 and Wimbledon singles champ eight times between 1927 and 1938.

"Big Bill" Tilden also was a standout in the sport of tennis. He was quite a figure both on and off the court. A handsome six-footer with a firm jaw and a loping walk, Tilden wore white flannel trousers and a V-neck sweater.

In 1920, Tilden became the first American to win the men's singles championship at Wimbledon. He was known for his powerful serve. He covered the back of the court with graceful steps and a huge reach. His

Few athletes have ever dominated a sport as Helen Wills (top) did tennis. Between 1927 and 1933, she won every set of every singles match she played. Bill Tilden (bottom) was the first U.S. man to win a Wimbledon singles championship.

pounding forehands and backhands wore down his opponents and forced them into errors.

In 1923, golfer Bobby Jones won the U.S. Open. In 1930, he won a historic "Grand Slam": the British and American amateur titles plus the British and U.S. Open crowns. No one has done it since. Many experts consider Jones to be the greatest golfer of all time.

Champion Swimmers

Early in this century, a person could become world famous by swimming across the English Channel (the body of water that separates England from France). On August 6, 1926, Gertrude Ederle became the first woman to swim the channel.

To prepare, she smeared on layers of grease from head to toe. This was to protect her from strong tides, choppy waves, and icy water. Ederle started near Calais, France, early in the morning. As she swam against a strong current, friends and reporters aboard two tugboats urged her to quit. "Why should I quit?" she hollered. She walked out of the water near Dover, England. The 35-mile channel swim took 14 hours and 31 minutes. Ederle broke the men's record by 1 hour and 59 minutes. Between 1921 and 1925, she held 29 amateur national and world swimming records.

The king of 1920s water sports was Johnny Weissmuller, a son of Viennese immigrants. For more than a decade,

he was unbeatable in swimming distances of 50 yards to a half-mile. He was the first swimmer to win five Olympic gold medals — three in the 1924 Olympics and two in the 1928 games. However, he is probably best known by Americans as the star of the early Tarzan movies. ■

Women athletes such as Helen Wills and Suzanne Lenglen were true pioneers. They opened the way for other women in professional sports. Do you think people today give as much respect to female athletes as to male athletes? Do you think women should be able to compete against men in certain sports?

Many experts consider Bobby Jones (left) to be the best golfer of all time. In 1926, 19-year-old Gertrude Ederle (below) became the first woman to swim the English Channel. She beat the men's world record by almost two hours.

TEST RACING RESULTS

The Sun

NEW YORK, FRIDAY, AUGUST 6, 1926.—

III.—NO. 286—DAILY.

PRICE THREE CENTS.

RTRUDE EDERLE SWIMS ENGLISH CHANNEL

NTS WIN SECOND STRAIGHT FROM REDS;

AMERICAN GIRL MAKES RECORD OF 14 1-2 HOURS

FOUR MORE AR QUESTIONED HALL INQU

Big Business

At one time, John D. Rockefeller's Standard Oil Company controlled 90 percent of the American oil business.

Leaders of American industry made fortunes at the beginning of the 20th century. An ambitious – and tough – businessman could make huge profits simply by controlling the manufacture and sale of a single product. To do this, businessmen formed trusts by putting together groups of companies that made the same product. The trust reduced the competition and set its own price for its product. These industrialists were called *robber barons* because of the methods they used.

In 1890, Congress passed the Sherman Antitrust Act, which made many of these trusts illegal and outlawed price-fixing. However, some businessmen managed to get around it. John D. Rockefeller, for instance, bought out his competition and became one of the richest men in the United States.

A Born Businessman

Rockefeller was a born businessman. The son of a New York salesman, as a child he is said to have bought candy by the pound and sold it at a profit to his brothers and sisters. In 1870, he formed the Standard Oil Company in Cleveland, Ohio.

Within only 12 years, Rockefeller controlled 90 percent of the American oil business. As he grew more powerful, he drove his competitors out of business and bought their companies at bargain prices.

Railroad Man

Another "big business" leader was J. P. Morgan. The son of a wealthy banker, Morgan enjoyed an easy life as a young man. Smart and full of energy, Morgan formed the International Harvester Company (now Navistar) and combined two other companies to form General Electric. He also formed U.S. Steel, the world's first billion-dollar corporation.

Morgan became the most powerful person in the railroad business. As a member of the board of directors of many American railroads, he formed a trust that controlled ticket and cargo prices across the country. This trust was later declared illegal by the U.S. Supreme Court and was dissolved.

Furious, Morgan visited President Theodore Roosevelt. Morgan was so sure of his power that he demanded, "If we have done anything wrong, send your man to my man and they can fix it up." Although the trust was dissolved, Morgan managed not to lose any money.

Muckrakers Scrape Up Dirt

As big business grew, so did the number of its critics. Magazines like *McClure's* were written by muckrakers, people whose writings uncovered corruption in big business and government.

Ida Tarbell, a writer for *McClure's*, set out to expose the dishonest practices of the Standard Oil Company. Some say she had a grudge against Rockefeller because he had forced her father out of business.

Tarbell researched Standard Oil for five years, using company records and proof of unfair practices gathered by other investigators. In the *History of the Standard Oil Company*, she wrote that Rockefeller had used bribes, false bookkeeping, and violence to dominate the oil industry. The book got a lot of publicity and, some say, led to federal action against the company. ∎

J. P. Morgan (above center) formed the world's first billion-dollar corporation. Muckraker Ida Tarbell (left) works at her desk. She wrote a book that exposed the corruption of Rockefeller's Standard Oil Company.

What does the phrase big business *mean to you? To some, particularly people who think big companies underpay workers, these are "fighting words." To others, big business means success and the American Dream. Take an informal poll of people you know. Ask them what they think of when they hear the phrase* big business. *Then write a paragraph about the different answers you get.*

Labor for Sale

While a handful of business leaders became rich, many Americans— especially immigrants—were mired in poverty. According to a 1906 report, more than 60 percent of American workers did not earn enough money to support a family. Having only their labor to sell, the poor in America included most factory and farm workers and almost all immigrants.

The "sweatshop" was a part of life for many immigrants who worked in cities. A sweatshop was a factory that also served as an apartment. Hours were long, pay was low, and working conditions were unsafe. Twenty or more employees often lived in the same apartment.

The average workweek in 1905 was 58 hours. A week's wage for the average worker in this period was about $25, though many—especially women and blacks—made less. As assembly lines were used more and more throughout industry, work became increasingly dull and, sometimes, dangerous. Accidents in factories were common.

Child Labor

Some sweatshop workers were children. For many of them, school was a luxury that their families could not afford. Nearly 2 million children under age 16 were employed in factories and fields in the early part of the 20th century. This was about 15 percent of the nation's schoolchildren. In 1900, one out of three workers in southern cotton mills was under age 16. Working

Young factory workers (above) picket for better pay and time off for school. Coal mines (right) hired many young boys to work for low pay.

hours and conditions were so severe that a 1907 law was passed to limit the time a child could work to 60 hours a week. This was considered humane.

After 12 hours on the job, children sometimes fell asleep at their work. This earned them a bucket of cold water in the face. Worse still, sleepy children sometimes got their fingers and hair caught in the machinery. Many were killed on the job. At that time, few companies set safety rules.

The Urban and Rural Poor

The poor in both factories and fields had little time for anything but work. Steelworkers had 12-hour workdays, six days a week. Sometimes they worked 16 or 24 hours at a time. In 1919, an unskilled worker at U.S. Steel earned less than $1,500 a year—just barely enough to feed, clothe, and shelter a family of five. Others earned much less. A maid earned about $7 a week, sometimes working 80 to 100 hours.

The living conditions of the poor were hardly any better. In cities, they were crowded together in small, dingy apartments that had little light or fresh air. The death rate for infants of the city poor was incredibly high—43 percent at the turn of the century. In the country, especially the rural South, few homes of the poor had an adequate roof or heat.

Unions Step In

To fight low wages and unbearable living conditions, workers had formed

One Woman's Story

Ella May Wiggins had nine children to raise. Alone. Her husband had been crippled in a work accident. He became an alcoholic and left her.

Her 60-hour week working nights in a cotton mill paid just enough to buy groceries. Her nine children grew up in rural North Carolina without shoes or medicine. Four of them died of whooping cough.

Ella May joined the union at the cotton mill and became a leader. During a strike in September 1929, she was murdered by a mob that shouted, "We're all 100 percent Americans, and anybody that don't like it can go back to Russia."

This boy (above left), who lost two fingers in a factory accident in 1912, received no compensation from his company. The people below were slum dwellers.

INDUSTRIAL WORKERS OF THE WORLD.
ORGANIZATION, EDUCATION, EMANCIPATION,
NEW YORK DISTRICT INDUSTRIAL COUNCIL
HEADQUARTERS 60 COOPER SQUARE.

The Industrial Workers of the World was one of the most radical unions of the times. The IWW found members among the poorest of American workers.

Martyr for Labor's Struggles

After he was shot by a firing squad, IWW organizer Joe Hill became the symbol of the labor movement's struggle. Hill had made a name for himself as a writer of workers' songs. He took the melodies of popular gospel hymns and rewrote them with words that antiunion people considered dangerous.

In 1914, he was accused of killing a grocer in Utah. Many believed that the charges were false and his trial was unjust. He was found guilty and executed in 1915. More than 30,000 people attended his funeral. Legend has it that Joe Hill's last words were "Don't waste any time mourning. Organize!"

unions. They attracted millions of members. The American Federation of Labor (AFL) demanded shorter hours and higher wages. Other groups, including the Industrial Workers of the World (IWW), fought for more extreme goals. The IWW wanted to end the pay-scale system and to overthrow capitalism.

The IWW was led by a towering figure, Big Bill Haywood. A mine accident had crushed one of his hands and left him blind in one eye. To workers, these injuries added to his power as a speaker and leader. The IWW found members among the poorest of American workers — especially migrant workers. Its members were called "Wobblies" and included a number of Communists. They carried red membership cards. Anticapitalist, antireligious songs were printed in the IWW's famous "Little Red Songbook."

The Wobblies quickly became the target of terrorist attacks. Conservatives feared a revolution like the 1917 Bolshevik Revolution in Russia, in which workers overthrew the government. Attacks against the Wobblies got worse during and after World War I. Strikes in southern and western states, often organized by the IWW, turned into bloodbaths more than once. ■

In your opinion, do unions still help fight social injustice in the United States? Would you support a union boycott (organized refusal to use or buy a product)? If your answer is "It depends"— what does it depend on?

Birth of Modern Consumerism

In 1920, raccoon coats were in – at least with college students from wealthy families. Coca-Cola was "keen," and *everybody* smoked Camels (they were only 2¢ a pack). For $2,885 you could drive away in a brand-new Cadillac and put an electric lighter in it for $5. At home you could use your new $48 vacuum cleaner or just sit back and listen to your phonograph, which cost $115 at Sears.

People bought more than they ever had before. During the 1920s alone, the gross national product (GNP), or total of all money spent in this country on goods and services, skyrocketed from $69.6 billion in 1921 to $103.1 billion in 1929. Through improved technology, industries could produce goods more cheaply. Consumers were eager to buy.

ADAMS Chiclets CANDY COATED GUM
10 for 5¢
CHICLETS CANDY COATED GUM

Libby's

WHEN NOT IN USE KEEP BOTTLE CLOSED IN A COOL PLACE
Libby's Salad (MAYONNAISE) Dressing

$20.00 FOR THIS
Made to Your Measure
ALL WOOL SUIT

We make every suit to your individual measures from the exact fabric you select and according to your exact specifications. We ship it on approval, delivery charges prepaid, for you to try on, to inspect and examine. Unless you are well pleased with your bargain your trial order will not cost you one cent. Write us today —

BIG CATALOG FREE

Send us a postal today for a copy of our big new catalog and style book with 65 cloth samples of the very finest, high grade fabrics
New York
you. We

Deal

Any memb
We guaran
risk. By
you save th
an

Choose from 65 Beautiful Patterns

The BELL Tailors

Sunset Khaki for Vacation

SUNSET SOAP DYES

Ridgways ORANGE LABEL Tea
FAMOUS BLEND OF INDIA-CEYLON BLACK TEA

Tea

AGENTS: $40 A WEEK
New Kerosene (Coal-Oil) Burner
Makes any stove a gas stove. Burns just like gas. Cheapest fuel known. Wonderful labor saver. Safe.

Free Sample to Workers

Pays for itself in a short time

No kindling to cut—no coal to carry—no ashes to empty. Everybody delighted with it. The high price of coal makes this burner sell everywhere. Agents just coining money. Write for Agency and demonstrating sample.
Thomas Burner Co. 901 Gay St. Dayton, Ohio

IVORY SOAP
99 44/100% PURE

Keeping Up with the Joneses

Meanwhile, advertising – on billboards, in newspapers, and later on the radio – made Americans hungry for things that used to be only for the rich. People bought things just to impress their neighbors; thus the saying "keeping up with the Joneses" came into the language. To spend, the advertising industry hinted, was to be a patriotic, modern American. In 1929, advertisers spent $3.4 billion on advertising – more than 3 percent of the GNP.

Buy Now, Pay Later

"Buying on time" quickly caught on with the American public. In 1926, Americans used credit to buy *$4.5 billion a year* in goods. By the end of the 1920s, consumers owed more than $6 billion. But today's numbers would surprise the consumer of the 1920s. At the beginning of the 1990s, American buyers used credit cards to charge *$12.5 billion per week* in goods and services! ∎

Common Items in the 1928 Home

In 1928, electric irons were found in most of the 27 million American homes. Other items included:

Radios	10 million homes
Vacuum cleaners	6.8 million homes
Washing machines	5 million homes
Electric fans	4.9 million homes
Electric toasters	4.54 million homes
Electric heaters	2.6 million homes
Electric refrigerators	755,000 homes

Source: U.S. Department of Commerce

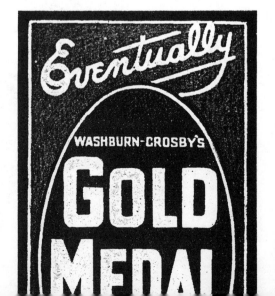

Digging Deep

Every April, many American taxpayers groan as they fill out their income tax forms. Did you know that the federal income tax is a fairly recent tax? Until the beginning of the 20th century, the federal government got most of its money from taxes on imported goods and interstate trade. But in 1913, the income tax was put into place by the 16th Amendment to the U.S. Constitution.

The United States had always had both very wealthy and very poor citizens. Many people felt that an income tax – especially if the rich were taxed at a higher rate than the poor – would be a fair way to even out the tax burden.

People opposed to income tax called it "socialistic." Socialism is a system in which a country's major industries and services are owned and distributed by the government. Many Americans feared "creeping socialism." The slogan "100 percent Americanism" was born in the early years of this century as an attack against socialist ideas.

Since 1913, the rules and rates of the federal income tax have changed many times. During World War I, the richest people were taxed up to 67 percent of their income. These rates were cut in half during the 1920s. ■

When income tax began, some people protested that the tax was "socialistic." Income tax rates and regulations are still controversial today. The picture shows a man who is "broke" after taxes.

Boom and Bust

October 29, 1929: Crowds gather outside the New York Stock Exchange on Wall Street. Investors had lost confidence in their stocks and were trying desperately to sell them at any price.

The Roaring Twenties blazed on, a decade on fire with hope and greed. The nation was "dry" because of Prohibition, but people were drunk with the lure of easy money and quick profit.

The economy was booming. This could be seen in cities where stores were stacked with the latest fashions and appliances. Wall Street, the heart of American business, was an exciting place to be in the 1920s, especially from 1927 to 1929. People who owned stock bought and sold shares through stock traders, called *brokers*.

Between 1927 and 1929, the number of shares of stock that changed hands doubled—from 577 million shares to 1.125 billion shares. By 1929, the average prices on leading stocks were five times what they had been in 1921.

But much of the "money" financing the boom did not really exist. Investors bought stocks "on margin," that is, with money borrowed from stockbrokers. By 1928, the amount of money investors owed their brokers was greater than the total of all the money circulating in the United States!

Moreover, before the 1920s, only a rich few "played the market." But by 1927, more than 1.5 million people were said to own stock. Most people, however, had no savings to invest in the stock market. This was certainly true of immigrants and workers.

By the end of the summer of 1929, there were signs that the boom was over. Stores were filled with goods that couldn't be sold. Construction had long

ORST STOCK CRASH STEMMED BY BANKS;
2,894,650-SHARE DAY
EADERS CONFER FINI

SWAMPS MARKET;

STOCKS GAIN AS MAR
BANKERS PLEDGE C
HOOVER SAYS BUSI

STOCKS COLLAPSE IN 16,410,030-SHARE
BUT RALLY AT CLOSE CHEERS BROK
BANKERS OPTIMISTIC, TO CONTINUE

With
for Steel.

his opinion on the poss...
...day's collapse in the stoc...
to his announcement, tne
detailed reports of st...

CLOSING RALLY

Trading u

TIRRED
BREAK

Proposal for
of Federal
System.

In stirring up interest in his
ing resolution offered last May
an investigation of the Federal
serve System. He said he would
sist upon action by the Senate Ba
ing and Currency Committee in
December session.

Immediate Inquiry Unlikely.

Senator Norbeck of South Dak
chairman of that committee,
clared that the committee appare
would favor an inquiry in the reg
session, but there was little pro
bility that it would be recommen
in the present session. At this
the Senate is absorbed in the t
bill

CKED

said:
become

since slowed down, and the prices of farm goods were dropping.

Black Tuesday

On October 29, 1929, the stock market crashed. Investors lost confidence in their stocks and desperately tried to sell them at almost any price. That day, stockholders "dumped" a record 16,410,030 shares of stock, causing losses of millions of dollars. The day became known as "Black Tuesday." The loss of money trickled down from wealthy investors to working people, who lost jobs and savings—and hope.

What caused the crash of 1929? One reason was foolish investing. Investors bought stocks not for what they were worth, but for what they thought they could sell them for. This practice, called *speculation*, led to rising prices and, finally, to a crash.

Other causes were agricultural; prices on farm products were unstable, and farm workers were fired. Fewer farm products were traded with foreign countries. "Protective" tariffs, or taxes on imported goods, raised the prices of imported goods by as much as 50 percent. This may have helped American industries temporarily, but Europeans and others soon stopped buying American goods.

In the meantime, Wall Street gains of the 1920s went mostly into the pockets of the wealthy 5 percent of the population, who received 30 percent of the nation's income. Salaries went up during this period, but the real buying power of workers and farmers either stayed the same or dropped. Advances in technology made factories more efficient, but they also put unskilled workers out of jobs. As a result, there were not enough people with money to buy the goods produced. A pattern of poverty and unemployment had been set.

Eventually, one-sixth of the population would be out of work. The U.S. government would experiment with the most radical program in its history to feed, clothe, and employ the 16 million people who had lost both jobs and hope. ∎

In 1929, investors could not see the crash coming. Do you think we would recognize the danger signs today? Read the business sections of a few recent newspapers. What are people saying about the state of the economy these days?

SOME KEY STOCKS:
The Week of the Crash

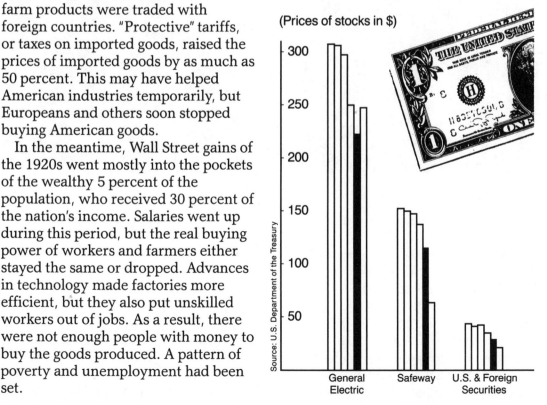

(Prices of stocks in $)

300
250
200
150
100
50

Source: U.S. Department of the Treasury

General Electric   Safeway   U.S. & Foreign Securities

Graph shows the drop in the value of three stocks between Thursday, October 24, 1929, and Wednesday, October 30, 1929. The black bar represents "Black Tuesday," October 29.

Were They Guilty?

Nicola Sacco (left) and Bartolomeo Vanzetti are shown here being led handcuffed from a courthouse. They were executed on August 23, 1927.

They died in the electric chair in Boston on August 23, 1927. Their case had dragged on for seven years. But Americans were still asking questions. Who *were* Nicola Sacco and Bartolomeo Vanzetti? Were they, as the judge called them, "anarchist bastards" who wanted to overthrow the American government by violence? Or were they just a "good shoemaker" and a "poor fish peddler" sentenced to die because they were immigrants with unpopular ideas?

Millions of Americans were ready to believe the worst about Sacco and Vanzetti. After World War I, many Americans began to fear and hate "foreign-born" people. Immigrants, they believed, were behind many of the day's troubles. People blamed immigrants for violent labor strikes, bomb throwings, and the rise of an

American Communist party, which had many foreign-born members.

Sacco and Vanzetti were arrested in 1920. They were charged with murdering two men during a robbery in Massachusetts. The trial was filled with conflicting stories and evidence. Gun experts told the jury that one of the murder bullets came from an automatic weapon owned by Sacco. The defense presented eyewitnesses to the holdup who claimed the two men had nothing to do with it. But after a six-week trial, the jury found Sacco and Vanzetti guilty.

Many people thought that the two men were convicted because they were anarchists—people who want to overthrow the government and do not want to put any other system in its place. From 1921 to 1927, Sacco and Vanzetti tried to get a new trial. They appealed to the state supreme court. At one point, a convicted criminal claimed *he* was the real murderer. But no court would overturn the conviction—and in April of 1927, Sacco and Vanzetti were sentenced to death.

To the end, each man claimed he was innocent. In a talk with the press shortly before he died, Vanzetti was reported to have said: "Never in our full life could we hope to do such work for tolerance, for justice, for man's understanding of man, as now we do by accident. Our words—our lives—our pains—nothing! The taking of our lives—lives of a good shoemaker and a poor fish peddler—all! That last moment belongs to us—that agony is our triumph." ■

THEN & **N**OW

The Sacco-Vanzetti case can still provide the "fuel" for a good argument. Whether the two men were guilty or innocent, the feelings of fear and hatred around them led to an unfair trial. In 1977, 50 years after their death, Massachusetts governor Michael Dukakis signed a proclamation that recognized the mistakes of the trial—and cleared the names of Sacco and Vanzetti.

Many thought Sacco and Vanzetti had been accused of murder because of their radical political beliefs. These people are protesting in support of the two men.

Scandals in Government

President Warren G. Harding, whose presidency was filled with scandals.

On February 2, 1924, a trembling Albert B. Fall came before a U.S. Senate committee and refused to answer any more questions about his part in a big oil scandal. Why did he make use of his right to remain silent? It was because what he would say could prove he was guilty.

Fall, who had once been U.S. secretary of the interior, was at the center of the first major government scandal of the 20th century. He would become the first former cabinet member in the country's history to go to prison. The scandal, called Teapot

Dome, became a symbol of dishonesty in American politics and big business of the 1920s.

"Normalcy" – and Scandal

The Teapot Dome scandal shocked Americans. Fall had been appointed by President Harding. Hadn't he promised a return to "normalcy" and less troubled times? America's idea of normalcy did not include the Teapot Dome scandal.

The scandal developed when Secretary Fall made a secret illegal agreement to let oil company owners take oil from land owned by the U.S. government. One of these oil fields was located at Teapot Dome, Wyoming.

When the deal was discovered, a Senate committee investigated and held hearings. Although it took a long time for the truth to come out, the men involved were finally brought to trial for breaking the law. Only Fall was sent to jail, convicted of the crime of bribery – taking money (in this case, from oil company owners) for doing something against the law. He was fined $100,000 and sent to prison for one year.

More Dirty Laundry

Teapot Dome was one of several scandals during the Harding administration. Another involved corruption of the Veterans' Bureau under Charles R. Forbes. During less than two years in office, Forbes was involved in the illegal sale of government supplies and in secret

President Harding and staff at a baseball game. Secretary of the Interior Albert Fall (right) was later sent to prison.

deals. He made a profit from the building of hospitals for war veterans. In January of 1923, Harding called Forbes to the White House to ask him to resign, but allowed him to leave the country first. Forbes fled to Europe and sent his resignation from Paris two weeks later. After he returned to the United States, Forbes went on trial in 1924 for planning to cheat the government. He was convicted and received a two-year prison sentence and a $10,000 fine.

Harding was greatly disturbed by the scandals that developed. He had trusted the people he appointed to office. When, for example, he was first told that people suspected Albert Fall of taking bribery money, Harding said, "If Albert Fall isn't an honest man, I'm not fit to be president."

On August 2, 1923, Warren G. Harding died during a trip to the western United States and Alaska. Some people believe his health was affected by the unfolding scandals.

Public Opinion

How did the American people react to the scandals? Public opinion forced several of the officials involved to leave their jobs. But at first, the people and the newspapers were angry with the senators and other government officials who had investigated the scandals. They didn't seem to be as angry at those who had cheated the government! In general, people seemed to think that giving so much attention to dishonesty was not good for the country or, at least, for business.

As the years went by, more and more details about the scandals were made public. But the information was confusing and hard for the average person to piece together. And by then, most Americans had lost interest.

Some historians say that if Warren G. Harding had been alive when all the corruption in his administration was uncovered, he might have been impeached – forced by the Congress to leave office. But not for another 50 years, until the presidency of Richard Nixon, did scandal force a president from the White House. ■

How much do you know about the Watergate scandal? It drove former president Richard Nixon from power in 1974. Ask several people what they remember about Watergate. Write up a few notes comparing people's memories of the scandal.

> "If Albert Fall isn't an honest man, I'm not fit to be president."
>
> – President Warren G. Harding

"The Crime of the Century"

Many people enjoy books and movies about "the perfect crime." It's interesting to see criminals plan a crime so perfect, so clever, that it *has* to work – without the criminals' getting caught. Although the idea of the perfect crime fascinates us, few people would actually try to commit one.

But in 1924, two Chicago teenagers wanted to prove they could get away with a "perfect" murder. Nathan Leopold, Jr., and Richard Loeb were excellent students. They both came from wealthy families. They seemed to "have it all." On May 21, 1924, however, they threw away their future. They kidnapped 14-year-old Bobby Franks and murdered him by hitting him on the head with a chisel.

The crime turned out to be far from perfect. Leopold and Loeb left plenty of evidence for police to find. Leopold, for example, left his eyeglasses at the scene of the crime. The police picked up the two boys for questioning, and they confessed to the kidnapping and murder of Bobby Franks. They were quickly brought to trial.

The crime horrified and sickened people all across the United States. It immediately became the biggest news story of the year. The *Chicago Tribune*, especially, wrote about it from every angle. The newspaper called it "the Crime of the Century."

Darrow's Defense

Leopold's and Loeb's parents hired a famous criminal lawyer, Clarence Darrow, to defend their sons. The two had already confessed to the bloody murder. Darrow had just one job – to save their lives. He wanted to get them a sentence of life in prison instead of the death penalty.

But how? Illinois punished brutal murderers with death, and Leopold and Loeb certainly seemed to deserve it if anyone did. Darrow was sure of one thing: the two boys were mentally ill and had been for years. He decided to base his defense on this.

According to Illinois law, lawyers could try to protect their clients from harsh penalties by showing that the penalties would be unfair. Darrow decided to try showing Judge John R. Caverly that the boys should not be executed, because of their mental illness. Darrow said, "The press calls my clients 'monsters.' Well, they *are* monsters – human beings without normal human feelings. For that very reason, they cannot be held completely responsible for what they have done."

When Darrow began to explain this defense in court, the prosecuting attorney quickly objected. He claimed that evidence about the boys' sanity couldn't be used because they had pleaded guilty. He maintained that such evidence could be used only to argue that defendants were not guilty by reason of insanity.

The judge considered this objection. If the judge agreed with the prosecution, Darrow's whole case would be ruined. But after three days, the judge decided he would listen to evidence about the boys' mental state before deciding how to punish them.

Psychiatrists for both sides then testified about Leopold's and Loeb's mental health. For almost a month, a battle between experts went on.

A Plea for Mercy

Darrow began his final argument on August 22, 1924. His speech may have been the finest plea for love and

Nathan Leopold, Jr. (front) and Richard Loeb (right) enter prison in 1924 to begin their life sentences.

understanding of his long career:

"[Leopold and Loeb] cannot feel what you feel and I feel . . . they cannot feel the moral shocks which come to men that are educated and who have not been deprived of . . . emotional feelings. . . . Is Dickie Loeb to blame because . . . he was born without [them]? If he is, then there should be a new definition of justice. . . . If I could

Clarence Darrow: With Infinite Pity

He defended Leopold and Loeb as well as John Scopes. He also defended war protesters after World War I; William D. "Big Bill" Haywood, a radical labor leader accused of assassinating a former governor of Idaho; and a black man who had fought off a mob trying to drive him and his family from their home in a white neighborhood of Detroit. Clarence Darrow was always there to defend an underdog or support a progressive cause. It's difficult to imagine U.S. law in the first decades of the 20th century without him.

Clarence Darrow, born in Ohio in 1857, was above all a champion of human rights. He took up the cause of workers, the poor, and people who found themselves in trouble with the law because they were weak or unlucky. He was a brilliant courtroom lawyer who could inspire a jury with his words.

Darrow was loved by the people he represented and respected by those who opposed him. Darrow's former law partner, Judge William Holly, said at his funeral: "In Clarence Darrow's heart was infinite pity and mercy for the poor, the oppressed, the weak, and the erring—all races, all colors, all creeds, all humankind. He made the way easier for many."

Clarence Darrow in action. A newspaper headline announces that Leopold and Loeb escaped the death penalty.

ever bring my mind to ask for the death penalty, . . . I would do it with the deepest regret that it must be done, and . . . with sympathy even for the ones whose lives must be taken. That has not been done in this case. I have never seen a more deliberate effort . . . to create . . . hatred [than] against these two boys."

On September 10, the judge sentenced Leopold and Loeb to life in prison. Darrow had won. He had saved his clients from hanging. They were immediately taken to prison.

Within a few days, the Leopold-Loeb case was off the front pages. The crime was now history. ■

Leopold and Loeb "got off" in part because of things that psychiatrists said about them in court. Throughout this century, people have been found "not guilty by reason of insanity." Today, some states allow a verdict of "guilty but mentally ill."

Do you think mental illness is a fair defense for people charged with serious crimes? Should it determine whether the person is found innocent or guilty?

How do you think someone judged "guilty but mentally ill" should be punished? Should the person go to a mental hospital, then go to jail after being "cured"?

THEN & NOW

The Leopold-Loeb case got people talking about capital punishment. Some were amazed that the two boys "got off," and criticized the judge harshly. Others pointed to the life sentences as proof that a kinder time was beginning in the United States. These arguments for and against the death penalty are the same arguments we hear today. Capital punishment continues to divide Americans.

Many people thought Leopold and Loeb should have been executed to set an example and to keep others from committing the same crime. Opponents argued, then as now, that no penalty can keep some mentally ill people from committing crimes.

Supporters of capital punishment also insisted that Leopold and Loeb should have been executed for a very different reason: they felt that only execution would satisfy the public and prevent people from taking the law into their own hands. In answer, opponents of the death penalty said that fear of mobs is a poor argument for execution.

Then, as now, people who favored the death penalty argued that it protected society. At the very least, the death penalty would make sure that dangerous criminals like Leopold and Loeb did not have a chance to repeat their crimes. Opponents answered that only a small percentage of all criminals are executed. They said that the wealth, education, or social class of a person might determine whether he or she receives the death penalty. In fact, some lawyers feel that Leopold and Loeb probably would have been hanged if their families had been poor.

Man and Monkey

It was more like a circus – or a county fair – than a trial. People poured into the usually quiet town of Dayton, Tennessee, in unheard-of numbers. Some drove old-fashioned wagons pulled by mules; others came in noisy Model Ts. Hot dogs and lemonade were for sale on the street. Reporters from all over the United States were there, too. The clack-clack of the telegraph mixed with the buzz of excited talk. Most incredible of all, big-city radio had come to Dayton: station WGN from Chicago was broadcasting the trial. It was the great "Monkey Trial" of 1925 – a lively battle between believers in science and believers in religion.

In March of 1925, the state of Tennessee had passed the Butler Act, a law about the theory of evolution. According to this law, no teacher in a public school could teach "any theory which denies the story of the Divine creation of man as taught in the Bible [and says] instead that man has descended from a lower order of animals." The Tennessee lawmakers were challenging "modern thinkers" to risk time in jail for their beliefs.

John T. Scopes, a high school biology teacher, took the challenge. He taught Charles Darwin's theory of evolution – that humans developed from "a lower order of animals" – to his students. He did this knowing he would be arrested and tried. He was one of a group of people who wanted to test the law. They wanted to get a court to rule on whether the law violated "free speech" rights, which are guaranteed by the U.S. Constitution.

So, in the intense heat of a Tennessee July, the trial began. If it was a circus outside the courtroom, it was a bitter fight inside. Two legal giants from outside Dayton fought this battle. William Jennings Bryan, famous speaker and politician, was the lawyer for the state. Clarence Darrow, fresh from the Leopold-Loeb case, defended Scopes.

A Great Battle

From the beginning, the two lawyers argued about more than the case. Bryan claimed that he was defending religious faith – fundamentalism, which means the belief that the Christian Bible is fact. Darrow said he

Biology teacher John T. Scopes listens to his sentence in 1925. He was found guilty, but was given a fine of only $100.

was defending free thought and modern science.

Near the end of the trial, something very unusual happened. Darrow asked Bryan to testify as a Bible expert. Darrow made Bryan look foolish by pointing out inconsistencies in the Bible. The trial had been moved outdoors, and a crowd of hundreds saw Bryan lose his temper time after time.

What was the outcome? Scopes was found guilty of breaking the law. But his punishment was very light: a $100 fine. Perhaps the judge who decided the sentence realized that the law was shaky.

Scopes's lawyers appealed the verdict to the Tennessee supreme court. The court reversed the conviction because it disagreed with the way the trial had been handled. But it did *not* rule on whether the law was constitutional, which was what Scopes and his lawyers had really wanted. So, in a way, neither side won. ■

Do public schools in your area allow prayer in the classroom?

Do you believe prayer and religious groups belong in the public schools? Why or why not?

THEN & NOW

The controversy behind the "Monkey Trial" is still going on, generations after John Scopes got a "slap on the wrist" from a Tennessee judge. In recent years, fundamentalist groups have worked to have "Creation Science" taught in schools. Creation Science is a set of ideas and theories that ties scientific explanations to parts of the Bible's creation story. Supporters of Creation Science say it should be taught side by side with evolution. Critics say it shouldn't be, because it isn't really science.

The Scopes trial goes on.

The Scopes trial (above left) was moved outdoors. A crowd of hundreds gathered to hear the legal battle. Inside the Dayton, Tennessee, courtroom, opposing lawyers Clarence Darrow (left) and William Jennings Bryan chat.

An Experiment That Failed

In 1917, the United States Congress passed an amendment to the country's Constitution – the 18th Amendment. By 1919, three-fourths of the state legislatures had voted for the amendment. In 1920, it became part of the law of the land. The era of Prohibition had begun.

The Prohibition amendment made it illegal to make, sell, or deliver alcoholic drinks. Its aim was to remove liquor from American life. A large group of Americans had dreamed of a country without alcohol for many years. They

"I Did It with My Little Hatchet": Carry A. Nation

Carry A. Nation was a leader in the fight to make drinking alcohol illegal. She died in 1911. But without her work, Prohibition might never have happened.

Nation had married a man who was an alcoholic. He died young, and she was left very poor. She blamed liquor for her troubles. She believed God was telling her to save the country by destroying saloons where men drank. In the late 1800s and early 1900s, Carry Nation wrecked saloons in many states. Almost six feet tall and very strong, Nation used bricks, rocks, and her famous hatchet to "bust" the saloons. She was often arrested. But her actions made many Americans think about the problems caused by liquor. She helped bring about the "no more booze" law of the 1920s.

DRYING UP Number of "wet" states
before National Prohibition

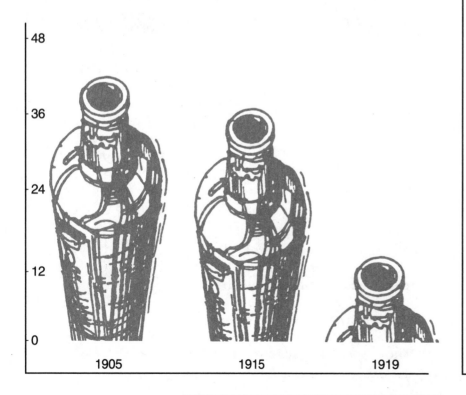

1905	1915	1919

thought that people would be better parents, spouses, and citizens if they stopped drinking. At first, many Americans liked the idea of Prohibition.

By the end of the 1920s, however, most Americans felt that Prohibition was a failure. Americans were actually drinking *more* alcohol than before. Many people broke the law by making "booze" at home. They drank illegal alcohol in secret nightclubs called speakeasies. They bought bottles from bootleggers—people who made or sold liquor and carried the bottles in loose-fitting boots. Breaking the Prohibition law became a game for many Americans.

People found that Prohibition meant *more* crime, not less. Gangs of criminals fought to control the liquor business in cities across the United States. Gang killings were very common.

Prohibition was another battle between "old-time" and "modern" America. In the end, the new thinking won: Prohibition was ended by Congress in 1933. Americans could drink again without breaking the law. ■

Prohibition officers pour illegal liquor into the sewer.

Medical Miracles

On average, babies born in the United States today will have a life span almost 30 years longer than that of their great grandparents born in 1900. Today's babies will also receive better health care – all thanks to the medical miracles of the 20th century.

One of these miracles was the victory over infectious disease. In 1900, parents had many diseases to fear. Thousands of children died of influenza (flu) and tuberculosis (TB). By 1929, the number of deaths from these two killers was greatly reduced. Scientists also battled other infectious diseases that killed children – scarlet fever, strep throat, diphtheria, whooping cough, and measles.

In the early 20th century, scientists and doctors began to find the causes of these diseases and to discover how they were passed from person to person. They then fought a two-front war. First, wherever possible, they prevented the disease from occurring. Then, if the disease did strike, they

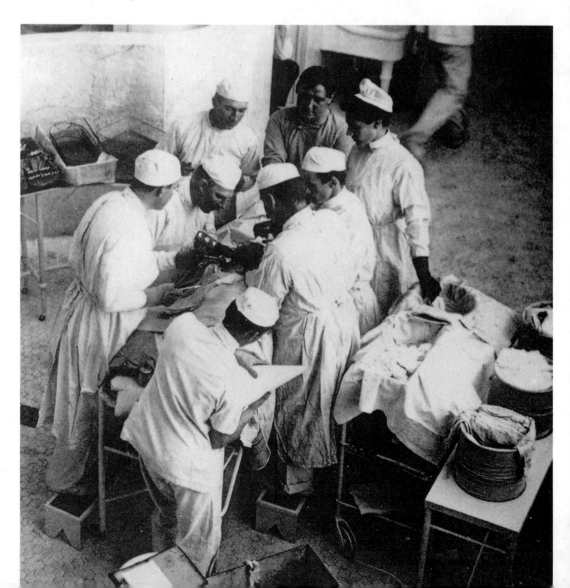

Surgeons operate on a patient in 1904. Surgery was much riskier then.

fought the disease itself.

For example, doctors discovered that certain mosquitoes carry diseases such as yellow fever and malaria. Health workers tried to wipe out the mosquito by spraying insect-killing chemicals in places where it lived. Fewer mosquitoes meant fewer deaths from these diseases. The death rate was cut further when doctors developed drugs to help those who did become infected with yellow fever or malaria.

The Lessons of War

Out of the evil of war can come good things: useful medical advances. World War I caused terrible suffering and loss of life. But during World War I, doctors and scientists learned lifesaving surgical methods that prevented infections. This greatly reduced the need to amputate, or cut off, infected body parts.

Other scientific discoveries also helped lengthen and improve life. In 1912, scientists found that we need vitamins – substances found in some foods – for normal health and growth. Within a few years, lack of vitamins had been shown to cause such diseases as scurvy, rickets, and beriberi. Vitamins, scientists found, cured and prevented these diseases. ■

The 20th century truly has been a time of medical miracles. Defeating diseases, improving surgery, and developing "wonder drugs" were just the beginning. But such advances cost money, and each generation has to decide if it wants to spend it.

In your opinion, should the government fund research into cures for diseases like cancer and AIDS? If not, how can money be raised to fight these diseases?

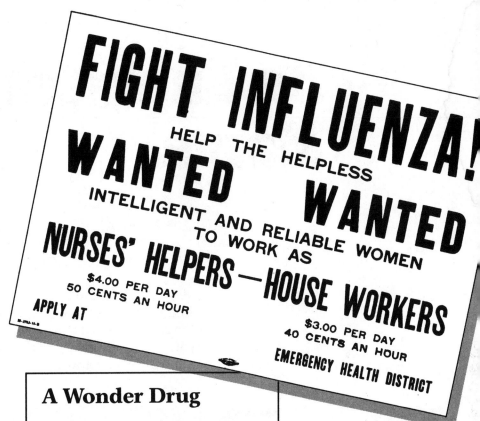

A Wonder Drug

"When I saw those bacteria fading away, I had no suspicion that I had got a clue to the most profound . . . substance yet used to defeat bacterial infections in the human body." The man who wrote these words was Scottish medical researcher Sir Alexander Fleming. He was referring to one of the most famous discoveries in the history of medicine: the discovery of penicillin. In 1928, Fleming was working on an experiment in his lab. Suddenly, some airborne mold landed in the dish he was using for his experiment. The mold immediately started killing bacteria. At first, Fleming did not realize the importance of his discovery. And it took many years before Fleming's discovery could be put to practical use. But by 1946, penicillin was saving millions of lives. Along with other "wonder drugs," it continues to save lives today.

> **Penicillin: "the most profound substance . . . to defeat bacterial infections"**
>
> — **Sir Alexander Fleming**

An Engineering Marvel

A MAN. A PLAN. A CANAL. PANAMA.

The words above are a famous English palindrome—a phrase that reads exactly the same forward and backward. Try it.

This palindrome is not just a word game. It is also a brief summary of the story of one of the most amazing engineering events of all time. The *man* was U.S. president Theodore Roosevelt. He set the stage for the thousands of workers who took part in the great project. The *plan* was to build a canal that would join the Atlantic and Pacific oceans. The *canal* was the Panama

Modern technology helps to clear the way for the building of the Panama Canal. After 10 years of labor, the Panama Canal opened on August 15, 1914.

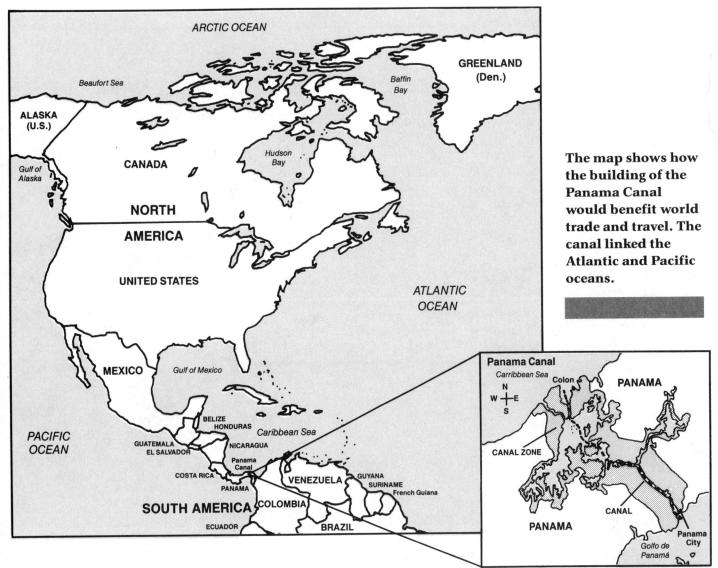

The map shows how the building of the Panama Canal would benefit world trade and travel. The canal linked the Atlantic and Pacific oceans.

Canal—an engineering marvel.

As the map shows, Panama is a narrow piece of land that separates the two oceans. If a boat could cross Panama, it would not have to go all the way around the tip of South America to get from New York to San Francisco. This shortcut could save weeks of travel and cut shipping costs. In the 1880s and 1890s, the French had tried to build a canal across Panama, but they had failed. In the early years of the 20th century, the United States decided to try.

In 1902, the United States bought the bankrupt French New Panama Canal company. However, the government of Colombia, which controlled Panama at the time, wouldn't agree to let the United States build the canal. When

rebels in Panama fought for independence from Colombia, the United States helped them. U.S. naval forces protected the rebels in their short, bloodless revolt. The nation of Panama was created in 1903. In the summer of 1904, the United States began work on the Panama Canal.

Linking Oceans

This canal would be 51 miles long. It would raise ships as high as 87 feet above sea level through a series of locks and channels. This would help ships move from one ocean to the other.

From the beginning, the planners of the canal knew they faced serious

The completed Panama Canal as seen from the bow of an American ship making its passage.

problems. The site is located close to the equator. The average temperature is 80 degrees Fahrenheit, and the average rainfall is 105 inches a year – a real jungle! When the French had tried to build a canal, nearly 20,000 workers had died from malaria and yellow fever.

By 1904, however, the United States had several advantages. U.S. Army doctors had learned how to fight yellow fever and malaria. Earth-moving and digging machines had become much faster and more powerful. Finally, the United States didn't have to start from scratch. It was able to use the French maps and plans.

Even with these advantages, the planners were not sure they would succeed. But after 10 years of labor, thousands of workers from up to 16

different countries did, indeed, succeed. The Panama Canal opened on August 15, 1914. ■

The Panama Canal was a great achievement – but it also got the United States involved in the politics and economy of Central America.

What is your opinion of U.S. involvement in Central America today? Did you approve of the invasion of Panama that overthrew Manuel Noriega in 1990?

According to the Panama Canal Treaty of 1977, the people of Panama will have complete control of the canal on December 31, 1999. How do you feel about this?

The Country Hits the Road

I will build a motor car for the great multitude. . . . It will be large enough for the family but small enough for the individual to care for. . . . It will be so low in price that no man making a good salary will be unable to own one. . . .
— *Henry Ford, October 1908*

This was a bold statement. But Henry Ford made good on it. The motor car Ford described was called the Model T. Within a few years, it completely changed the way Americans traveled. Soon, the automobile was no longer a toy for the rich; instead, it became a "must" for millions of average Americans.

Cheap, Rugged, Versatile

What was it about the Model T that made it so popular? First, as Ford promised, it was cheap. It cost around $1,000 — about half the cost of most cars. Within a few years, Ford had even lowered the cost by 60 percent.

Second, it was durable and easy to maintain. Steel alloys made the Model T strong and rugged. Repairs were simple and quick because the "T" used standardized parts.

Third, the Model T was versatile. Its body rode high above the ground, so it was ideal for bumpy country roads. And with a top speed of about 45 miles per hour, it could make excellent time on the new paved roads.

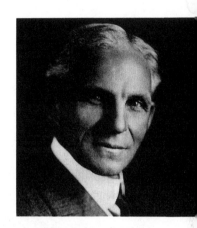

Henry Ford (above) helped change the way Americans traveled. His factories built millions of Model Ts. A few of these automobiles are shown rolling off an assembly line (left).

Henry Ford built his cars with strong steel alloys. Though the bridge under this Model T collapsed, the car suffered only a few broken spokes on one wheel.

A New Way to Build Cars

In 1909, Ford made about 10,000 Model Ts. In 1916, his company made more than 1 million. To up car production, Ford completely changed the way cars were made. He developed the world's first continuously moving assembly line in his Highland Park, Michigan, plant during 1913 and 1914. By bringing parts to the assembly workers, the line helped workers put Model Ts together faster and better. Ford called this "mass production."

Mass production wasn't completely new. But Ford's mass-production method was different. As he said, it involved "power, accuracy, economy, system, continuity, and speed." Other industries tried to use Ford's mass-production method for making furniture or building houses. They soon found that it didn't work. In fact, by the late 1920s, the Model T kind of mass production didn't work for Ford either. By then, car buyers looked for new and different models each year. Ford's mass production worked only for making the same car year after year. When buyers started looking for different types of cars, *flexible* mass production replaced Ford's method.

Mass-produced automobiles brought cheap, dependable transportation to millions of American families. These cars made it possible to work in the city and live in the suburbs. And the American landscape of today—with highways and freeways linking city, suburb, and countryside—is the direct result of cars like Ford's Model T. ■

Imagine life before the automobile. List different ways that the automobile has changed people's lives.

Into the Wild Blue Yonder— and Beyond

December 17, 1903, was a cool, cloudy day in Kitty Hawk, North Carolina. Only a few dozen people gathered to see Orville and Wilbur Wright try out their latest invention—a flying machine. Orville flew their wooden plane only 100 feet or so. It stayed in the air for only about 12 seconds. Then everyone went home. Few people realized that they had seen a historic event: the first controlled flight of an engine-powered aircraft.

For five years, most people didn't know or understand what the Wrights had managed to do. The newspapers didn't take the Wrights seriously until 1908, when the brothers successfully demonstrated their improved Wright Flyer. In 1909, when crowds of more than one million in New York City watched Wilbur Wright's demonstration flights, the public finally understood the Wrights' achievement.

The Wright Flyer, 1903, takes off in the first motorized airplane flight.

Charles Lindbergh climbs into an open-cockpit airplane in the 1920s. In 1927, Lindbergh became world-famous for his nonstop flight across the Atlantic Ocean.

Air Travel Spans the Globe

During and after World War I, improvements made airplanes fly higher, faster, and longer. In 1923, the first nonstop cross-country flight was made in just under 27 hours. (This trip was recently completed by a U.S. Air Force SR-71 aircraft in just over one hour.) Soon, airmail service began. By the late 1920s, airplanes were carrying passengers.

On May 20, 1927, a young airmail pilot named Charles Lindbergh set out to fly nonstop from New York to Paris. A little over 33 hours later, he thrilled the world when he landed safely at Paris's Le Bourget Air Field. Airplanes had proven that they could span the globe.

Rockets Blast Off

Just two years later, in 1929, Lindbergh sat in the home of Robert Goddard. Goddard had quietly started the modern age of rocketry in 1926. Lindbergh listened to Goddard outline his ideas for the future of rockets. Lindbergh would live to see Goddard's ideas take men to the moon and back, 40 years later.

In the 1920s, though, the future for rockets did not look good. Before then, they were little more than toys or fireworks. Unlike aircraft, rockets had not played an important role in World War I. And after the war, when new accomplishments in aviation seemed to take place daily, rocketry had yet to get off the ground.

But on March 16, 1926, Goddard launched the first liquid-fueled rocket. It used a mixture of gasoline and liquid oxygen. The rocket flew for only 2½ seconds, rose 41 feet high, and traveled just 184 feet. Like the Wright brothers' first flight, it was not very impressive. But Goddard's rocket was the basis for all future space flight, including today's space shuttle. ■

Robert Goddard poses with his rocket in 1926. His use of liquid fuel is the basis for modern space travel.

Charles Lindbergh was a great American hero of the 1920s. Do we have any heroes like him today? Think of someone who is a hero to you because of his or her accomplishments. Why do you admire this person?

Thirty Seconds to Disaster

On April 18, 1906, at 5:13 A.M., the residents of San Francisco, California, suddenly felt as if the world had lost its balance. Within a matter of seconds, a powerful earthquake reduced much of the city to rubble. In minutes, fires had sprung up around the city. They soon grew into fierce blazes that caused even more destruction and death. The quake and the fires killed as many as 700 people. The entire downtown area was destroyed. About 250,000 were left homeless.

At 5:04 P.M. on October 17, 1989, minutes before the San Francisco Giants were to play the Oakland Athletics in a World Series game, another major earthquake rocked the San Francisco Bay area. Although millions more people lived in the bay area in 1989, only 63 people died in the 1989 quake. And although San Francisco had many more buildings in 1989, there was much less destruction. In fact, most buildings were not damaged. The tragedy of 1906 helped teach everyone how to better survive the quake of 1989. ■

I was sure the house would fall down before I got out. It rocked, like a ship on a rough sea.

— Exa Atkins Campbell
San Francisco, 1906

Every time I rose from the couch, the shaking pulled me down again. The building leaped, and everything in my room came crashing down.

— Alice Legare
San Francisco, 1989

The Widening World

By 1900, one of the last unexplored parts of the world was the North Pole. The challenge to be the first to the pole was taken up by American naval officer Robert E. Peary. The quest to reach the North Pole was Peary's greatest goal. But success did not come easily. Twice Peary tried – and failed – to reach the North Pole, in 1898 and 1905. On the second try, he almost succeeded. But difficult sledding conditions and bad weather forced his team, including Matthew Henson and four Eskimos, to turn back. During these attempts, Peary and his team suffered frostbite, sickness, and years of separation from family and friends.

Peary did not give up. On March 1, 1909, Peary and his party began a third try for the pole. Weather conditions were not promising. A howling wind and temperatures of –50 degrees Fahrenheit met the men as they left camp. But on April 6, 1909, Peary and his team reached 90 degrees north latitude – the North Pole!

Soon after reaching the pole, Peary wrote in his diary: "My life work is accomplished. The thing which I intended from the beginning that I should do, the thing which I believed could be done, and that I could do, I have done. I have got the North Pole out of my system." ■

American naval officer Robert E. Peary was the first person to reach the North Pole. After two unsuccessful attempts, he and his team reached the pole in 1909.

Titanic Tragedy

CHICAGO DAILY NEWS

TUESDAY, APRIL 14, 1912.

ONE CENT ... 37TH YEAR.

SEVENTH EDITION

TITANIC, WITH 1,341 PERSONS, LIES AT BOTTOM: ONLY 868 ARE SAVED

MEN OF FAME DEAD IN DISASTER IS FEAR; LIST OF THE RESCUED

HOW WOMEN AND CHILDREN WERE SAVED.

ALL HOPE ABANDONED; HELP CAME TOO LATE; BRINGING SURVIVORS

...hia Sends Word That His

Everything seemed so peaceful aboard the great ship, the *Titanic*, on the night of April 14, 1912. Musicians had stopped playing for the night on the first-class deck. Stylish men and women had returned to their cabins for the night. The fourth day of the ship's first voyage—from England to New York—was almost over. There would not be a fifth day.

Rich and Poor

The 1,320 passengers and 900 crew members on the *Titanic* were making history. It was the largest ship ever built. It was also the most luxurious. It had beautiful furniture and a magnificent Grand Ballroom. The passenger list included many famous Americans, including multimillionaire John Jacob Astor and Archie Butt, a close aide to President William Howard Taft.

Far below the first-class cabins, however, was a different type of passenger. The third-class section carried more than 700 persons. Many of them were European immigrants on their way to a new life in the United States.

Rich and poor alike, however, had

every reason to feel confident about their ship. The *Titanic* had been built with a special design that people said made it unsinkable. Engineers boasted that watertight compartments, far below the ocean's surface, would keep the *Titanic* afloat—no matter what.

Perhaps the crew of the *Titanic* were too confident. On April 14, they had received many warnings from other ships about huge icebergs floating in the cold but quiet waters of the Atlantic. Just before midnight, the *Titanic* struck an iceberg. For about 10 seconds, the enormous frozen mountain scraped and bumped along 300 feet of the ship's right side, deep below the waterline.

The Great Ship Goes Down

Many crew members and passengers felt only a slight shaking. But serious damage had been done. Water was pouring into the ship. The glorious voyage was about to become the world's most famous disaster at sea. Within three hours, the "unsinkable" *Titanic* would sink. More than 1,500 men, women, and children would die.

At first, most passengers did not think the damage was serious. But the

A newspaper reports the sinking of the Titanic. Notice that the next-day numbers of the dead and the survivors are close to the actual numbers—but too optimistic.

The *Titanic* leaves on its first voyage on April 10, 1912, four days before it sank.

captain ordered all passengers on deck, where the ship's band played to help keep people calm. Although crew members were assigned to help women and children into lifeboats, the transfer did not go smoothly. Many people didn't want to get into the lifeboats. The huge *Titanic* still seemed much safer than the small boats swinging over its side. Sadly, many of the boats were not filled when they were lowered over the side. And there were not enough lifeboats for all the passengers anyway.

An hour after the collision, the first lifeboats were lowered. At 2:05 A.M., the last lifeboat touched the calm ocean waters. Fifteen minutes later, the forward bow of the *Titanic* tilted deep into the sea. A deafening roar was heard as furniture and equipment broke loose and went sliding and crashing inside the ship. Finally, the *Titanic* slipped into the sea.

The 705 survivors were picked up from their lifeboats within hours by the *Carpathia*, a passenger ship passing nearby on a voyage from New York to the Mediterranean Sea. The *Carpathia* turned around and headed back to New York, where a stunned nation waited to hear the story of the sinking of the *Titanic*. ■

In the 1990s, a few survivors of the Titanic *were still alive. They were children when the great ship sank. If you could talk with one of these people, what would you ask her or him? Make a list of questions you would ask in an interview.*

THEN & NOW

Almost immediately, efforts were begun to find and recover the *Titanic*, the victims, and the ship's treasures. Many plans were considered, but the cost and the lack of equipment and know-how made the job impossible.

In 1984, however, research groups in France and the United States quietly began planning to explore the area where the ship went down. An expedition was launched, led by Dr. Robert Ballard. On September 1, 1985, an underwater craft equipped with a camera and special lights discovered the *Titanic*.

When Ballard returned to Washington, D.C., to report on his findings, this is what he said:

"The *Titanic* itself lies in 13,000 feet of water on a gently sloping alpine-like countryside overlooking a small canyon below.

"Its bow faces north and the ship sits upright on the bottom. Its mighty stacks point upward. . . .

"It is quiet and peaceful and a fitting place for the remains of this greatest of sea tragedies to rest.

"May it forever remain that way and may God bless these found souls."

* This symbol before a page number indicates a photograph of the subject mentioned.

Credits

Photo Credits

The Alan Mason Chesney Medical Archives of the Johns Hopkins Medical Institution: 80

Courtesy American Jewish Historical Society, Waltham, MA: 47

The Bettmann Archives: 2b, 3a, 8, 9, 11, 12ab, 22abc, 23, 29, 30, 31ab, 43a, 44ab, 48, 57ab, 58, 59a, 60a, 61a, 62, 66, 73, 74, 77ab, 79, 90

Courtesy of the Trustees of the Boston Public Library: 68, 69

Robert Brautigan, Norwich, CT: 26

Broadcast Pioneers Library: 39, 40

Courtesy Chicago Bears: 53

Chicago Historical Society; SDN 62,959: 52a

From the Collection of the Texas/Dallas History and Archive Division, Dallas Public Library: 45

Denver Public Library, Western History Department: 49

Frank Driggs Collection, New York, NY: 43b

Courtesy the Statue of Liberty, Ellis Island Foundation, Inc.: 19

From the Collections of Henry Ford Museum and Greenfield Village, Dearborn, MI: 85ab, 86

By permission of the Houghton Library, Harvard University: 41

International Tennis Hall of Fame and Tennis Museum at The Newport Casino, Newport, RI: 56ab

Courtesy Elizabeth Johnson, Red Bluff, CA: 33

The Kansas State Historical Society, Topeka, KS: 78

Reprinted with special permission of King Features Syndicate, Inc.: 16

Courtesy Mariners Museum, Newport News, VA: 10, 92

Courtesy MetLife Archives, New York, NY: 81

George Herwig Collection, Midcoast Aviation/Missouri Historical Society, St. Louis, MO: 88a

Minnesota Historical Society: 42b

Museum of Modern Art/Film Stills Archive, New York, NY: 2a, 34b, 36ab, 37ab, 38ab

National Baseball Library, Cooperstown, NY: 50ab, 51, 52b

The National Portrait Gallery, Smithsonian Institution: 70

Courtesy of The New York Historical Society, New York, NY: 18, 21

Cover drawing by Rea Irvin; © 1925, 1933, The New Yorker Magazine, Inc.: 46a

Ida Tarbell Collection, Pelletier Library, Allegheny College, Meadville, PA: 59b

Courtesy Mrs. J.W. Petree, Anadarko, OK: 27

Princeton University Library: 42a

Reprinted by permission of the Reader's Digest Association, Inc. © 1991: 46b

San Francisco Maritime National Historical Park: 89a

Charles W. Stein Collection, Buffalo, NY: 34a, 35ab

Theodore Roosevelt Association: 7

United Press International: 76, 89b

University of Illinois at Chicago, The University Library, Jane Addams Memorial Collection: 25, 61b

University of Illinois at Urbana-Champaign: 55

U.S. Army Infantry Museum, U.S.A.I.C., Fort Benning, GA: 71

Courtesy Deborah Weise: 65

Courtesy Dorothy M. Weise, Chesapeake, VA: 32

Western History Collections, University of Oklahoma Library: 54

Oscar Whilden, Vine Grove, KY: 84

Woodrow Wilson Birthplace Foundation, Inc., Staunton, VA: 13

Courtesy Wright/Patterson AFB Museum, Dayton, OH: 3b, 87, 88b

Text Credits

Quotation on page 7 from *The Jungle* by Upton Sinclair. Penguin Books USA Inc.

George Burns quotations on pages 34 and 39 reprinted by permission of The Putnam Publishing Group, Inc. Copyright © 1989 by George Burns.

The Lee DeForest quotation on page 40 reprinted from *This Fabulous Century 1920–1930*. By the Editors of Time-Life Books. © 1969 Time-Life Books, Inc.

Poem excerpt on page 44 from *The Weary Blues* by Langston Hughes. Copyright © 1926 by Alfred A. Knopf, Inc., and renewed 1954 by Langston Hughes. Reprinted by permission of the publisher.

Excerpt on page 89 of letter by Exa Atkins Campbell courtesy Mr. and Mrs. James Atkins Tarver.

Quotation on page 90 from *Peary: The Explorer and the Man* by John Edward Weems. Copyright © 1967 by John Edward Weems. Reprinted by permission of Houghton Mifflin Co.